CIRCA 1903

CIRCA 1903

NORTH CAROLINA'S OUTER BANKS AT THE DAWN OF FLIGHT

LARRY E. TISE

UNIVERSITY OF NORTH CAROLINA PRESS CHAPEL HILL

This book was published with the assistance of the
Fred W. Morrison Fund of the University of North Carolina Press.

Manufactured in the United States of America
Designed by Richard Hendel
Set in Utopia, Madrone, and Sveva fonts by Tseng Information Systems, Inc.
The University of North Carolina Press has been a
member of the Green Press Initiative since 2003.
Cover illustrations: (*front, top*) Wright brothers' camp near Kitty Hawk,
courtesy of Library of Congress; (*front, bottom*) Wright brothers on fishing trip,
courtesy of Special Collections and Archives, Wright State University; (*back*) reporters
covering the Wright brothers' attempts at flight, courtesy of Harry Ransom Center,
University of Texas at Austin
Library of Congress Cataloging-in-Publication Data
Names: Tise, Larry E., author.
Title: Circa 1903 : North Carolina's Outer Banks at the dawn of flight / Larry E. Tise.
Description: Chapel Hill : The University of North Carolina Press, [2019] |
Includes bibliographical references and index.
Identifiers: LCCN 2018049778 | ISBN 9781469651149 (pbk : alk. paper) |
ISBN 9781469651156 (ebook)
Subjects: LCSH: Outer Banks (N.C.)—History. | Outer Banks (N.C.)—
Description and travel.
Classification: LCC F262.O96 T57 2019 | DDC 975.6/1—dc23
LC record available at https://lccn.loc.gov/2018049778

To the honor and memory of those several platoons of colleagues and friends who introduced me to and explained the ways of life and culture of North Carolina's barrier islands and its inland sea:

Herbert Paschal and Bill Still

Gertrude Carraway

Gordon Watts, Leslie Bright, and Richard Lawrence

Stanley Riggs

David Stick and Bill Harris

Carolista Baum

Keats Sparrow

Lois Pearce Smith

lebame houston

Darrell Collins

E. Thomson Shields and Charles Ewen

Sarah Downing, Tama Creef, and Stuart Parks II

Doug Twiddy and Clark Twiddy

Rita Seelig Ayers,

and the faculty and students of East Carolina University's Program in Maritime Studies with whom I have pursued many maps, mysteries, shipwrecks, and other submerged objects and artifacts from circa 1976 to the present

CONTENTS

CIRCA 1903

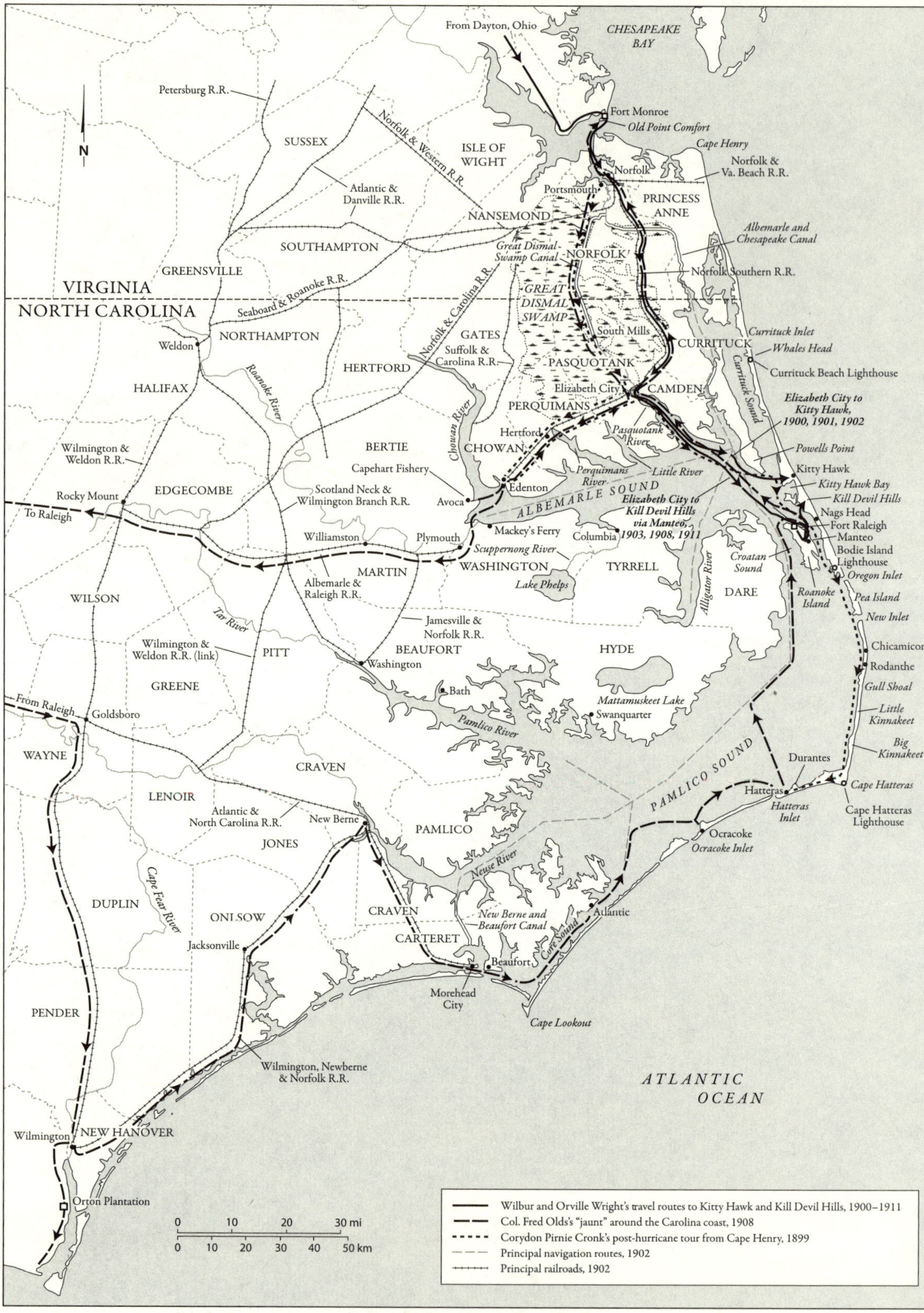

The Carolina coast and its inland sea, circa 1903

PROLOGUE

NORTH CAROLINA'S "OUTER BANKS"

Circa 1903 is a historical photographic record of a new world (for them) discovered by Wilbur and Orville Wright when they went to the coast of North Carolina for the first time in 1900 for the purpose of inventing flight. But this is not another book about the Wright brothers. It is rather about the Carolina coast as the Wrights encountered it: a place more surprising, complex, and suited to their purposes than they had ever anticipated.

The coastal region that became the Wrights' natural laboratory for aerial experimentation extended from the Virginia border southward to Ocracoke Inlet on the North Carolina coast and from Cape Hatteras on the east side to the farthest edge of navigable waters in the Albemarle and Pamlico Sounds on the west. North Carolina's distinctive barrier islands in this region face the Atlantic Ocean on their eastern sandy-beach sides. But these islands also form the natural perimeter for the shallow, mucky, but rich sounds. This inland sea was populated long before Europeans arrived and built the tiny port towns, scores of fisheries, and dozens of hunt clubs the Wrights encountered. There were hundreds of square miles of forest lands surrounding submerged outcroppings of cypress forests, vast stretches of dismals and swampy pocosins, and numerous mysterious freshwater lakes. It was a habitat fished, plied, and hunted by Indian nations for thousands of years and then by European interlopers—doing many of the same things as Indians had—from the 1600s, across four centuries before the Wrights arrived. This vast interconnected coastal world is the principal focus of this book.

In this book, I also seek to explain why the Carolina coast was the way it was when the Wright brothers first went there. Whereas the European settlers who gathered there from the days of Sir Walter Raleigh had looked toward the Atlantic Ocean as their link to the world's markets, by 1903 these Carolinians had largely forsaken the idea of creating a tidewater port across the barrier islands. They had become much more focused on the sound country as a passage to the mainland, making it into a realm that could operate with the same patterns of work and life one might find around the long perimeters of the Great Lakes in North America. With the active aid of the U.S. government following the American Civil War, the Carolina coast by 1903 possessed an extensive and well-oiled network of canals and railroads, lighthouses and river lights, weather and lifesaving stations, post offices and shipping stations. The place was such a marvel of precision and reliability that commercial promoters in the area proudly announced to the rest of America that the Carolina coast was open and ready for business.

It seems the Wright brothers had not gotten that message before they went to the Carolina coast, where they hoped to find a place to solve what was broadly understood at the time as "the problem of flight." They had recently learned from the National Weather Bureau that they could expect at Kitty Hawk the sustained winds of twenty miles per hour they were seeking and an abundance of soft sands to withstand many anticipated crashes. But the historical record suggests they knew little else about the place and were befuddled when they arrived. Once they learned the local ropes and understood the world they had entered, however, it turned out to be a marvelous place to build, modify, and test increasingly sophisticated flying machines. They went to the Carolina coast with an abundance of ideas and found a place where their dreams could come true.

It is probably best to clarify at the outset why there is a difference between the treatment of terms in the title of this book and some of the terminology used throughout. Except in rare instances, readers will not find the term "Outer Banks" much used in this book. That is because the now-familiar term "Outer Banks of North Carolina" had not yet been invented by the year 1903. Thus if one is going to attempt to portray the "sand banks" or the "barrier islands" of North Carolina—as they were called circa 1903—and use pictures from that period to show how these places looked, it does not make much sense to call North Carolina's coastal islands by names that were not used at the time.

For readers who know little about the lore of coastal Carolina, the absence of the term "Outer Banks" in this book will probably not be of particular importance. But it might come as a surprise to some newcomers and even to old-time Carolinians that this term and other cherished word handles applied to coastal Carolina history had not yet been coined by 1903 or for decades afterward. The term "Graveyard of the Atlantic"—now commonly used to describe the treacherous regions around North Carolina's coast—Cape Hatteras, Cape Lookout, and Cape Fear—was not in vogue at the time. Nor had the legend of "The Lost Colony" fully emerged by 1903. While many people—especially Carolinians—were aware that Sir Walter Raleigh had attempted to establish a colony on the coast of North Carolina in the 1580s and that it had disappeared, the transformation of this tragic error of the colonial past into an epic story of history, literature, and drama had not yet occurred.[1]

To avoid potential confusion, then, let it be said that this book is not really about "The Outer Banks of North Carolina" but rather it concerns "the outer banks of North Carolina." It focuses on a period some years before many crafty and well-meaning promoters—either homegrown developers or newly arrived land speculators—created the tourist mecca that would eventually become known far and wide as "The Outer Banks." And that leaves aside an even cozier, trademarked branding tool for the outer banks—"OBX"—that emerged much later still.

Along those same lines, we will not make any particular hullabaloo about the much-heralded "First Flight" of the Wright brothers on 17 December 1903. That term, too, was a later innovation coined by creative, well-intentioned historians and publicists seeking to attract tourists to the Carolina coast. The actual "first flights" of the Wright brothers occurred in September and October 1902 when the brothers accomplished more than 250 free, controlled flights of up to 622 feet and over periods of up to 26 seconds in duration. Those flights were without an engine. But that was actually the moment when the brothers knew they had flown and were confident that they had solved the problem of flight. Believing in 1902 that they had unraveled the mysteries of flight, they filed their application for a patent on their flying machine nine months before their first powered flight in 1903.[2]

It has always been a misleading piece of promotional shorthand to celebrate the powered flight of Orville Wright on the morning of 17 December 1903 as the world's "first flight." It takes a batch of delimiting terms to accurately describe the historical nature of that flight. The official version used by the National Air and Space Museum of the Smithsonian Institution describes it as a "free, controlled, and sustained flight" in "the world's first power-driven heavier-than-air machine."[3] Orville Wright's description of the flight required even more words. It was, he wrote, "the first [flight] in the history of the world in which a machine carrying a man had raised itself by its own power into the air in full flight, had sailed forward without reduction of speed, and had finally landed at a point as high as that from which it started."[4]

So how can one prepare to look at a place in an earlier period of time—a time that cannot simply be relived or physically reproduced? We are very fortunate in the case of attempting to see what the Carolina coast looked like in the years surrounding 1903. Several young individuals made their way to North Carolina's barrier islands around this time, toting tripod cameras and making photographs of what they saw and did while visiting. How some of them got to the area are stories unto themselves.

Corydon Pirnie Cronk (1859–1903), chief of the U.S. Weather Bureau at Cape Henry, Virginia, ventured to the Carolina coast in 1899 to record the devastations of one of the largest hurricanes ever to hit North Carolina—the San Ciriaco storm of August that year. The crisp photographic record of storm damage made by Cronk, a native of Michigan and a graduate of what is now Michigan State University, is one of the finest visual records of the Carolina coast at the turn of the twentieth century.[5]

Herbert H. Brimley (1861–1946), the first director of what was called the North Carolina State Museum, also started going to the coast in the 1890s to photograph wildlife, their habitats, and the livestock of North Carolina farmers. A taxidermist by training and eventually a renowned ornithologist, Brimley also collected photographs taken by others, which are blended with his own images in the State Archives of North Carolina and the North Carolina Museum of Natural Sciences.[6]

Frederick A. Olds (1853–1935), founder and first director of the companion North Carolina Hall of History, was also an avid collector of photographs that are now housed in both the State Archives of North Carolina and the present North Carolina Museum of History. A prolific travel writer and storyteller, Olds frequently made a photographic travelogue to accompany his stories.[7]

There were other photographers—many whose names are no longer associated with the pictures they took—who went there around 1900 to take pictures of North Carolina's lighthouses, lifesaving stations, sand dunes, forests, people, and much else. Their images remain in rich archival collections at the Outer Banks History Center in Manteo and sometimes blended into such varied assemblages there as that of Daniel Victor Meekins (1897–1964), newspaper editor and Dare County sheriff, himself a talented photographer.[8]

Among the greatest photographers of the era for the Carolina coast were the three brothers Lorin, Wilbur, and Orville Wright, who ventured to Kitty Hawk and Kill Devil Hills for six seasons between 1900 and 1911. Between the three of them, they not only made a meticulous visual record of experiments in flight; they also made indelible pictures of the surrounding environment. Although Lorin (1863–1939), the oldest brother, is often overlooked, his photographs are among the finest in the Wright collections at the Library of Congress and at Wright State University in Dayton, Ohio. Moreover, the three brothers wrote hundreds of letters and diary entries about what they encountered, leaving a rich written record of the coastal world they saw.[9]

The wide-ranging Wright collections also include some images made by a variety of visitors to the brothers' camps at Kitty Hawk and Kill Devil Hills. Among them are those of George A. Spratt (1869–1934), a medical school graduate and flight pioneer from Coatesville, Pennsylvania, who spent weeks with the brothers at Kill Devil Hills in 1901, 1902, and 1903. The most famous of all the photographs in the Wright collections is, of course, the classic image of the brothers' first powered flight on the morning of 17 December 1903. John T. Daniels (1873–1948), a crew member at the adjacent Kill Devil Hills Life-Saving Station, was recruited by the Wrights on the spot to click the shutter. Although he had never touched a camera before, we will always know that his timing on that occasion was perfect. His role in snapping one of the most renowned photographs of the twentieth century made him a local celebrity for the remainder of his life. Wherever he went after the Wrights released this photograph in 1908, Daniels was accorded instant honor. His lifelong association with the Wrights continued until the day of his death. Daniels died the day after Orville's demise in Dayton in 1948, and local newspapers featured side-by-side headlining obituaries for the two individuals connected to the world's first powered, controlled flight.[10]

The Wright brothers' penchant for secrecy surrounding their flight tests provided strong magnets for news photographers to chase them after 1903. Although the brothers carefully sequestered most of their own photographs for fear that rival aeronauts might learn too much about the design of their flying machines, the world became curious about what the Wrights were doing.[11] When they returned to Kill Devil Hills for more experiments in 1908 and 1911, they attracted a variety of photojournalists eager to get pictures of their flights for the world's highly competitive newspapers and magazines. James H. Hare (1856–1946), one of the world's most renowned members of this new profession, was commissioned by *Collier's Weekly* in 1908 to take the first clandestine photograph of a Wright plane in flight.[12] Van Ness Harwood (1873–1933), a reporter for Joseph Pulitzer's flamboyant *New York Herald*, got a similar assignment in 1911 when the Wrights introduced a new form of unpowered flight known as soaring. Writing and taking pictures for the *New York Herald*, Harwood replicated the visual record made by Hare three years before.[13] Both Hare and Harwood found their prey, but they also made other memorable images of the people and places they saw while on the Carolina coast.

Drawing on these vivid historical images, let's put ourselves for a moment in the position of the Wright brothers in August 1900. Wilbur has done his homework about the weather conditions at Kitty Hawk through the U.S. Weather Bureau in Washington. Based on that information, he has just written a letter to the keeper of the U.S. Weather Station at Kitty Hawk and is eagerly awaiting a reply. Increasingly certain that he and Orville are going to go to North Carolina to test and verify some of their ideas about flight, the bookish Wilbur probably turned to the only thing like a comprehensive and accessible data source for geography and history in their father's ample library—the *Encyclopedia Britannica*. If he did, the general index of the latest edition of the *Britannica*, the ninth, contained no references to Kitty Hawk, Kill Devil Hills, Nags Head, Manteo, or Elizabeth City—the places the brothers most needed to know about. The only reference to North Carolina at all led the reader to volume 17 (originally published in 1884), which had a general entry on the state written by "Prof. W. C. Kerr, late State Geologist, Raleigh, N.C., now of the United States Geological Survey, Washington, D.C."[14]

As might be expected from his experience in both geology and cartography, Kerr gave a brief description of the "physical features" of the Carolina coast. It was "diversified by numerous and extensive sounds, bays, rivers, lakes, marshes, swamps, and islands, the whole surface for 50 miles inland . . . less than 20 feet above sea level." "The sea," he continued, "is walled off from this low-lying territory by a long linear chain of sand-islands or dunes, ranging from 75 to 100 feet upwards in height." Harking back to North Carolina's huge aboriginal population, Kerr noted that "Indian corn occupies the largest acreage" of agricultural production in the state—surpassing both cotton and tobacco. Also noting the powerful heritage of the coastal region, Kerr indicated that "the fisheries of the eastern rivers and sounds are large and profitable—which is also what brought Indians to the area." And, finally, "the getting of lumber, both in the pine forests and in the cypress and juniper swamps, has been an important source of profit since its first settlement."

But Kerr also gave a brief foretaste of what might be in the offing when the brothers headed to Kitty Hawk. "In ten years the number of miles of railroad has been nearly doubled," Kerr wrote. Just as importantly from the view of the Carolina inland sea, he continued, "There are 1000 miles of waterways open to steamboat navigation, including rivers, bays, sounds, and canals, forming a nexus of lines of communication extending over the whole eastern and seaboard region and connecting with the various ports along the coast from Wilmington [North Carolina] to Norfolk in Virginia." Looking at the foldout map of North Carolina with the encyclopedia entry, Wilbur and Orville could pore over the section that showed the train route from Norfolk to Elizabeth City. There was no indication of steamboat connections across the watery expanse from there to Kitty Hawk, nor any guidance on the kinds of people they would encounter when they arrived. Even if the brothers turned to the then-current edition of the *Rand McNally Atlas* with its latest "New Map of North Carolina, 1894," they would have gotten no more insights into where they were headed.[15]

Just before Wilbur departed for the first time to Kitty Hawk in September 1900, he got two letters from Kitty Hawk—one from the weather station, written by the weatherman Joseph Dosher, and another from one of the most prominent residents of Kitty Hawk—the former postmaster—William J. Tate. Although these letters provided only small bits of additional information, they were encouraging to the brothers. Therefore, just days later Wilbur left Dayton by train to head toward Norfolk, Virginia. There he would transfer to another train that would take him to Elizabeth City. Wilbur went ahead first and alone, to be joined in a few weeks by Orville. And there our journey also begins.

Corydon Pirnie Cronk at the Cape Henry Weather Station (Cape Henry, Virginia, 1899). *Showing him at his official weather station desk, this photo was taken about the time Cronk made his photographic expedition to the Carolina coast following the San Ciriaco hurricane of August 1899. Photograph, photographer unknown, 1899 (Carol Cronk Cole Personal Collection). (Although this print has been damaged over time, it captures the essence of this devoted early meteorologist.)*

Herbert H. Brimley, first curator of the North Carolina Museum of Natural Sciences (Raleigh, ca. 1903). *Brimley, in this photo portrait, seems to be exhibiting both his stately manner and some of his works in his taxidermy lair in Raleigh, ca. 1903. Photograph, photographer unknown, ca. 1903 (PhC42 Bx6F20, Brimley Photograph Collection, State Archives of North Carolina, Raleigh).*

Colonel Fred Olds as a young man (Raleigh, date unknown). *In addition to collecting historical items and artifacts for display in North Carolina's original Hall of History, Olds was a prolific essayist and newspaper correspondent who wrote vivid descriptions of his travels in North Carolina, taking photographs to accompany his many published stories. Photograph, photographer unknown, n.d. (19XX.469.1a, Photo Collections, North Carolina Museum of History, Raleigh).*

Victor Meekins, reporter, photographer, and photo collector in a self-portrait (Manteo, ca. 1911). *As a teenage photographer, D. Victor Meekins took many images of coastal Carolina and collected many more for preservation. As a reporter for the* Elizabeth City Independent *from 1922 to 1927, sheriff for Dare County from 1927 forward, and as editor and publisher of Dare County's first homegrown newspaper, the* Dare County Times, *from 1935 until his death, Meekins was both an observer and an actor in virtually all public projects for the remainder of his life. Rarely did he go abroad without his camera. Photograph, self-portrait (PC.5126-13-50, D. Victor Meekins Collection, Outer Banks History Center, Manteo).*

James H. Hare, in a self-portrait (Manteo, May 1908). *As one of America's first renowned photo journalists who covered both wars and scientific explorations, including early flight, Hare routinely made photographic self-portraits to illustrate his exploits. He took this one (note tube from his right hand to his camera), posing as a fisherman in a small boat tethered to a dock in Manteo. Lantern slide, James H. Hare, 1908 (15102.624, James Hare Collection, Harry Ransom Research Center, University of Texas at Austin).*

Looking for a map of North Carolina in 1900—the *Rand McNally Atlas* (atlas map, 1894). *When Wilbur Wright determined through correspondence with the U.S. Weather Bureau that Kitty Hawk, North Carolina, was the only place on the East Coast that had the wind characteristics needed for flight—sustained winds of twenty miles per hour in one direction—his best sources for locating the place would have been the most recent edition of the* Encyclopedia Britannica *or the trustworthy* Rand McNally Atlas *with its latest "New Map of North Carolina." "A New Map of North Carolina, 1894," Rand, McNally and Company (Cm912 1890r, North Carolina Maps, 614, North Carolina Collection, University of North Carolina at Chapel Hill).*

1

EARTHSCAPE AND CLIMATE

"I chose Kitty Hawk because it seemed the place which most closely met the required conditions," Wilbur Wright wrote his father, Bishop Milton Wright, on 9 September 1900. Inscribing his first letter from North Carolina on the stationery of the Hotel Arlington at Elizabeth City, the elder of the two Wright brothers who invented flight explained why the tiny fishing village on the Carolina coast provided the perfect place for conducting "practical experiments" on what he called "the flying question."[1]

"At Kitty Hawk which is on the narrow bar separating the Sound from the Ocean," he continued, "there are neither hills nor trees, so that it offers a safe place for practice." Besides "the wind there is stronger . . . and is almost constant"—sufficient, he believed, to lift from the ground a controlled, man-carrying flying machine. What he called "the required conditions" at Kitty Hawk had been confirmed to him by both the world's foremost authority on flight at the time—Octave Chanute—and the U.S. Weather Bureau. Those required elements included several crucial items: sustained winds in one direction of twenty-one miles per hour; soft sands for many inevitable crashes; remoteness from the prying eyes of big-city newspaper reporters; and reliable transportation access from Dayton, Ohio. No other place known to either Chanute or the Weather Bureau contained all those factors the Wrights sought as their most permanent laboratory for testing several modes of flight.[2]

But neither Wilbur Wright nor his brother Orville had ever flown in an airship or a flying machine nor even attempted to make any kind of device—other than a kite—that would fly. Nor had they ever seen an ocean—much less the kind of barren, sandy, windswept barrier chain of islands they were about to experience for the first time on the coast of North Carolina. Wilbur described Kitty Hawk as unduly remote—even to the people in Elizabeth City. "No one seemed to know anything about the place or how to get there," Wilbur told his family.

Eventually, he got passage from Elizabeth City to the place with a local fisherman on a "flat bottomed," "half rotted," and "vermin-infested" boat that barely withstood, he thought, the high waves and surging currents of the treacherous waters between the mainland and Kitty Hawk Bay. He was certain that the skipper, one Israel Perry, was incompetent—that the man could neither command his shabby boat properly nor capably ply what Wilbur perceived as the stormy seas of the vast Albemarle Sound. Wilbur thought it almost a miracle that he had survived the dangerous voyage.[3]

Finally arriving on the sliver of sandy and scruffy land between the normally calm Albemarle Sound and the surging waves and tides of the Atlantic Ocean, Wilbur and Orville Wright in 1900 began their experiments. Despite the distance from their orderly Ohio home, the unpredictable patterns of weather, swarming hordes of bloodsucking mosquitoes, roaming armies of hungry pigs, sand-filled shoes and blankets, chilling nor'easters, walloping hurricane-force winds from the south, and every other surprise of raw nature and guileless men, the brothers Wright forged ahead—still unsure about their testing grounds.

When he got across the Albemarle Sound to Kitty Hawk on 11 September, Wilbur was welcomed as an out-of-state guest and as a temporary boarder at the home of William J. and Addie Tate. The Tates' small clapboard and wooden-shingle house served doubly as their family residence with their young daughters Irene and Pauline and as the official U.S. Post Office for Kitty Hawk, North Carolina. Being able to perch for three weeks in a local home was a godsend for the young man from Ohio.[4]

His hosts possessed the inherited ways in which coastal people—Indians and immigrating Europeans—for thousands of years had coped with their unusual world. It was an environment that was inviting when the weather was fair and hellish when winds and storms and ripping tides lashed across the narrow threads of sand. During the day Wilbur worked in the barren yard of the Tate house, cobbling together the first Wright flying machine. In the evenings he sat at supper with the family, hearing about the wild animals that lurked across the scraggly land and the ways humans withstood the persistent assaults of weather, sand, and biting insects. This initial encounter with the Tates would never be forgotten. The Tates remained lifelong friends and advocates of the Wrights and their pioneering flights on the Carolina coast for the remainder of their lives.

Bill in particular later styled himself as an official guide to the Wright brothers' Carolina coast and promoted in both North Carolina and Washington, D.C., the creation of a monument marking the most important site of America's first powered flights.[5]

When Orville arrived almost three weeks later, the brothers supped on duck and rabbit and fish—standard local fare in those parts—with the Tates and listened to more coastal lore until 4 October, when they ventured on their own into nature. For the next nineteen days, the brothers—inexperienced as campers—felt they had mounted a wild and unpredictable steed. They set up a tent on a sandy hill half a mile from the Tate home—roughly halfway between Kitty Hawk, a cluster of houses on the sound side of the banks, and the Kitty Hawk Life-Saving Station on the Atlantic shore side. To their consternation, their tent was blown down repeatedly by winds ranging from thirty to forty-five miles per hour. They took their first flying machine, a smallish device, out and tried to fly it as a kite. That worked well. They then tethered it by ropes to a wooden derrick they had built for testing the craft. But the flying machine was thrashed around and upended whenever they tried to work with it. Although Wilbur built the machine to carry five times his weight, it would not carry him aloft when it was flown as a glider. Adding insult to injury, the machine crashed and was left in a heap of broken rubble when crosswinds threw it into a dune known as "Look Out Hill," which the brothers renamed the "Hill of the Wreck."[6]

But all was not lost. When the machine would not lift Wilbur's 130 pounds, along came a small boy, Tom Tate (a nephew of Bill Tate). He was "a small chap [70 pounds] . . . that can tell more yarns than any kid of his size I ever saw," said Orville. The crude flying machine rose with the diminutive Tate aboard without difficulties. But when the smallish dunes at Kitty Hawk sometimes lacked the constant winds they sought, the brothers moved four miles southward to the much larger Kill Devil Hills. There, they found both perfect winds and an open terrain more suitable for flight. These large dunes—near no town, but adjacent to the Kill Devil Hills Life-Saving Station—became the locale for all the brothers' tests in their subsequent trips to the Carolina coast across the next eleven years.[7]

In addition to reckoning with the gusting and swooping winds, the brothers also began to understand the earthscape of the place where they hoped to fly. "But the sand!" exclaimed Orville. "The sand is the greatest thing in Kitty Hawk, and soon will be the only thing," he prophesied. Kitty Hawk was once "a fertile valley, cultivated by some ancient Kitty Hawker," he thought. He and Wilbur could see the results of recent shifts in the sands in the landscape of rotted limbs—once belonging to proud trees—

that protruded from the sand. "The sea," he observed, "has washed and the wind [has] blown millions and millions of loads of sand up in heaps along the coast, completely covering houses and forest." One night a "45 mile nor'easter" struck their camp and "took up two or three wagon loads of sand from the N.E. end of our tent and piled it up eight inches deep on the flying machine we had anchored about fifty feet southwest." While this was happening, the sides of their tent snapped repeatedly, sounding "exactly like thunder."[8]

While the Wright brothers marveled at the moving landscape of their test grounds, a young geology professor at the University of North Carolina in Chapel Hill, Collier Cobb, attempted to explain the ebb and flow of sands on the barrier island chain for the *National Geographic Magazine* in 1906. According to Cobb, the advancement of sands and the formation of great new dunes around 1900 was the result of years of people denuding the pine forests that had flourished on the Carolina banks for eons. "This movement of the sand was started just after the Civil War by the cutting of trees next to the shore for ship timbers," he wrote. He found that an entire fishing village on Hatteras Island had been buried by sand near a spot known as The Great Woods—where "not a stick of timber stands upon it today." Cobb's assessment of the changes was the best guess in an era that lacked essential data on the rise and fall of oceans that would be available to scientists a century later.[9]

Aside from the constantly shifting sands, one of the other fundamental modifications in the shape of the Carolina coast was the never-ending creation and melting away of inlets from, and thereby outlets to, the Atlantic Ocean across its barrier islands. The island chain experienced by the Wright brothers in 1900 looked nothing like the coast that had been encountered by the explorers sent to the same region by Sir Walter Raleigh three hundred years earlier. In fact, when Raleigh's explorers first arrived in 1584, the island chain between what would become the Virginia border and the Oregon Inlet contained at least four additional inlets that would be long gone by 1900: Currituck, Musketo, Carthys, and Roanoke. Musketo Inlet disappeared in 1671. Currituck was replaced by a new Currituck Inlet around 1713. Oregon Inlet evaporated in 1770 but then reemerged in 1846. Well before Oregon reopened, all the other inlets of the upper banks region had closed seemingly for good: Carthys and Roanoke in 1811 and the New Currituck in 1828. But a major shift in the banks occurred in 1846 when Oregon Inlet reopened. A new inlet that took the name Hatteras also appeared then for the first time in recorded history. By 1900 there were only three principal openings between the Atlantic Ocean and North Carolina's vast body of sound waters—Oregon, Hatteras, and Ocracoke—all three constantly being furrowed and maintained by the skills of government engineers.[10]

But since all these inlets for salty ocean waters were also outlets for North Carolina's freshwater rivers, the opening and closing of the inlets also had important implications for both the natural and the geopolitical development of the Carolina coastal region. First, the closing of the old inlets meant that North Carolina's tiny port towns no longer had natural barely navigable outlets to the sea. The inlets were never deep enough for seagoing vessels to pass through easily anyway. Even Sir Walter Raleigh's explorers three centuries earlier had used small, shallow-bottomed pinnaces to transport people and cargo across the banks to Roanoke Island. Nevertheless, a modest seagoing trade emanated from Edenton, Bath, and New Bern during the colonial era. It continued in a limited manner until the inlets of the upper banks closed in the early nineteenth century. Although small vessels were used primarily in a vibrant coastal trade that ranged from Boston to Florida, by the time of the Civil War, even these shallow craft could hardly make it to sea.

In the post–Civil War period when the U.S. government was flexing its engineering muscle all along America's coasts, North Carolina politicians and entrepreneurs constantly lobbied Congress and the U.S. Army Corps of Engineers to deepen the channels through Oregon, Hatteras, and Ocracoke Inlets. An expensive project to dredge a channel through Ocracoke Inlet was completed in 1897. But in a demonstration of the futility of attempting to alter the forces of nature, two years later the channel had shoaled, leaving the upper reaches of the Carolina coast without a single navigable channel to the sea, even for shallow coastal craft.[11]

A second consequence of the closing of the inlets was a much happier one for people who admired observing or plucking fish and fowl from one of the world's richest natural habitats. Whereas the Atlantic's salty waters had spilled into the sounds through porous inlets twice daily with the rise and fall of every tide, the disappearance of these water channels transformed the upper banks region of North Carolina—the Albemarle Sound—into a gigantic freshwater sea. As one of the largest freshwater habitats in America, the Albemarle became a lush environment for the growth of wide spans of the grasses beloved by migrating fowl. In the process, this inland sea became a perfect laboratory where the Wright brothers could study the behavior of soaring and swooping birds in flight. The seasonal shifts of millions of duck, geese, and other migratory birds from Canadian to South American habitats made the inner side of the Carolina's barrier islands one of the richest sites for the targeting of waterfowl in the Americas.

Another result of the closing of the inlets was a modification in the fish and shellfish culture of coastal Carolina. The transformation of the Albemarle Sound into a freshwater environment meant that its population of shad, herring, and striped bass exploded. Every February through April thereafter millions upon millions of these and other freshwater species could be harvested without depleting the abundance. But the disappearance of salt water north of Roanoke Island also meant that these waters could no longer produce oysters. Indeed, when North Carolina in 1887 commissioned a study of its coastal waters for the purpose of expanding the cultivation of oysters, its principal scientist excluded the entire Albemarle Sound region from its survey of existing oyster beds. But the presence of an abundant resource of fish and other sea life, ready to be harvested, was one of the defining characteristics of coastal Carolina at the turn of the twentieth century.[12]

While the opening and closing of inlets along the Carolina coast had a profound effect on the natural habitat of the region, by the first years of the twentieth century the presence or absence of these natural openings between sound and sea had little effect on the lives and habits of coastal Carolinians. As residents of one of the most constantly changing environments on the American coast, lifelong habitués of the region adapted to the changes. Sharing information on changing channels for boating and fishing, locals adjusted to the moving barrier islands, the relocation of fish and shell beds, and access to the Atlantic for saltwater fishing. There was no need in 1900 to build highways or bridges or to operate a fleet of ferries to convey vehicles from island to island. The daily experience of coastal residents was a water-based lifestyle and existence. Everyone proudly possessed a boat. The appearance or disappearance of an inlet at this time made little difference.

The barrier islands lacked the natural solidity or permanence to sustain a railroad bed. Thus no entrepreneur or public official ever dreamed of attempting to lay down a highway or byway that would depend on constant maintenance or an enduring firmament on the surface of the earth. Besides, when all was said and done, this was an environment principally consisting of water, wind, and sand. There were always methods of plying the waters. And everyone, resident and visitor alike, knew at the time that it was better to travel on water away from the ocean than to risk becoming thrashed on one of the shoals that lay outside the banks around Cape Hatteras or Cape Lookout or just about anywhere along the dangerous Atlantic coast.

Although neither Wilbur nor Orville graduated from high school, they were quick learners who adapted rapidly to their newfound coastal environment. They became accustomed to seeing cattle and wild ponies roaming across some of the grassy expanses around Kitty Hawk. They expected to encounter from the outset the sudden appearance at their camp of marauding pigs perpetually rooting for edibles not yet consumed by human beings. As the Wrights lofted their experimental flying machines into the complicated flux of air over Kitty Hawk, they also became experts in the acquisition and use of meteorological information. As keen observers of climate, they made daily calculations on wind, barometric pressure, and temperatures. They saw the mighty power of winds, storms, and furious seas that could move mountains of sands across the thin Carolina barrier islands. They saw trees that had been humbled by constant winds bowing away from the torrential blasts of air. They endured both hurricanes and tropical storms as they learned to turn nature on the continental fringe into an asset for inventing flight.

When storms were not brewing, they noted more pleasant spectacles of their ocean environment: "The sunsets here are the prettiest I have ever seen," observed Orville. "The clouds light up in all colors in the background," he continued, "with deep blue clouds of various shapes fringed with gold before. The moon rises in much the same style, and lights up this pile of sand almost like day."[13] Finding a kinship with his newly discovered natural workshop, Wilbur wrote his sister Katharine somewhat nostalgically as he and Orville left the coast for the first time in 1900: "We have said 'Good bye Kitty, Good bye Hawk, good bye Kitty Hawk, we're gwine to leave you now.'" With what they had learned about this fragile but volatile coast, about the people who lived there, and—most important—about themselves, they would be able to return for years, better prepared to take advantage of one of best places on earth for flying.[14]

Porch at the Kitty Hawk Post Office and home of William J. and Addie Tate (Kitty Hawk, 1900). *Wilbur and Orville Wright were fortunate to be hosted on their first trip to Kitty Hawk by William (Bill) and Addie Tate. Bill (*seated left with daughter Irene on his lap*) was a local gadfly and promoter of the virtues of the banks region of North Carolina and became a lifelong friend of the Wrights. Addie (*seated right with daughter Pauline standing by her*) was the postmistress of Kitty Hawk in 1900. The brothers (Wilbur, Orville, and Lorin) were expert photographers using a tripod camera and glass plates to make their photographs. By exposing to light a photo emulsion they spread on the plates, they captured images such as this one—but they did not know what the image would be until they returned to their home photo lab in Dayton, Ohio. This glass plate and many others in their collection were damaged or broken during a 1913 flood that inundated the basement storage area of their Dayton home. Glass plate negative (broken and damaged), Wright brothers, 1900 (L546, Wright Brothers Collection, Library of Congress). (For an analysis of this photograph and the many details contained in its nooks and crannies, see Larry E. Tise,* Hidden Images: Discovering Details in the Wright Brothers' Kitty Hawk Photographs, 1900–1911 *[Charleston: History Press, 2005], 19–20.)*

The Wright brothers' first Kitty Hawk experiment—tenting (Kitty Hawk, 1900). *After spending nearly a month as guests in the Tate home, Wilbur and Orville (who arrived several weeks later) moved to their 1900 campground (4–23 October) on top of a sand hill about half a mile outside of Kitty Hawk toward the Atlantic Ocean side of the island. Inexperienced at camping on a windswept mound of sand, the brothers innocently positioned their canvas tent making use of short wooden pegs in an exposed environment. After several nights of howling winds, they learned that they needed to reinforce their tent with a rigid frame, use much larger anchors, and tie it to a nearby tree. Glass plate negative, Wright brothers, 1900 (L549, Wright Brothers Collection, Library of Congress).*

The Wright Brothers' second Kitty Hawk experiment—flying (Kitty Hawk, 1900). *Not only did the Wrights fail initially at tenting; they also could not get their 1900 Kitty Hawk flyer to remain in the air in the turbulent Kitty Hawk winds. The machine went out of control while being tested as a kite and crashed into a pile of broken pine ribs and cloth (shown in this image) on what they named the "Hill of the Wreck." A few outlying buildings of the Kitty Hawk Life-Saving Station can be seen near the ocean surf in the background. Glass plate negative (slightly damaged), Wright brothers, 1900 (L544, Wright Brothers Collection, Library of Congress).*

A better place to fly—Big Kill Devil Hill, four miles south of Kitty Hawk (Kill Devil Hill, ca. 1902). *When the Wrights found that the winds at Kitty Hawk were insufficiently constant and the sandhills there too short for further experiments, they decided to explore the much taller dunes at Kill Devil Hills, about four miles south of Kitty Hawk. As revealed in this photograph from 1902, Big Kill Devil was a mysterious sight, from a distance having the appearance against the flat sandy plain of a tall mountain. Photograph, Wright brothers, ca. 1902 (15-7-16, Wright Brothers Collection, Paul C. Dunbar Library, Wright State University, Dayton, Ohio).*

"Millions and millions of loads of sand . . . covering houses and forest" (Kitty Hawk, 1900). *As the Wrights looked for places near Kitty Hawk to conduct their test flights, they charted in photographic form this juxtaposition of new sand blown against the sturdy Kitty Hawk woods (shown here) often after sand covered houses and forests, as well as the puddling of rainwater on flat terrain on the sound side of the barrier island (their 1900 machine is barely visible at the extreme right of this photograph). Glass plate negative, Wright brothers, 1900 (L561, Wright Brothers Collection, Library of Congress).*

Denuded pine forests permitted sand movements, thought one geologist (Kitty Hawk, 1906). *The intrepid march of sands across the "sand reef" and the pristine woods at Kitty Hawk was described by the Chapel Hill geologist Collier Cobb as the creation of "whale heads," a local term for newly emerging sand dunes that pushed across the banks. This image appeared with Cobb's analysis of the problem in the article "Where the Wind Does the Work" in the June 1906 issue of* National Geographic Magazine. *Lantern slide, photographer unknown (Cobb?), ca. 1906 (10003087-LS 3081, Photo Collections, North Carolina Museum of Natural Sciences, Raleigh).*

The diminishing number of inlets in the upper banks region, 1795. *By 1795 the number of inlets in the banks had diminished dramatically from the era of the earliest Europeans' explorations. New Currituck, Roanoke, and Gant inlets still permitted salt water into the Albemarle Sound. But neither Oregon nor Hatteras inlets had yet been carved out by the forces of nature. Only Ocracoke Inlet was sufficiently deep in the 1790s to accommodate ships of moderate draft. Detail of Samuel Lewis, "State of North Carolina from Best Authorities," 1795 (MC.150.1795, North Carolina Maps, 151, State Archives of North Carolina, Raleigh).*

North Carolina's coastal inlets are creations of capricious nature (Nags Head, 1899). *Inlets on the Carolina banks have always been capricious creations of the forces of nature—never entirely predictable. Massive storms such as the San Ciriaco hurricane of 1899 have frequently breached some of the thin and low-lying sections of the banks, closing old inlets and opening new ones—such as the "New Inlet" south of Nags Head portrayed in this image by Corydon Cronk during his journey along the banks in September 1899. Although the major inlets and thus outlets through the banks that would remain throughout the twentieth century—Oregon, Hatteras, and Ocracoke—were in place by 1900, they could be maintained only through mechanical dredging operations performed by the U.S. Army Corps of Engineers. Photograph, Corydon Pirnie Cronk, 1899 (AV.5138, Carol Cronk Cole Collection, Outer Banks History Center, Manteo).*

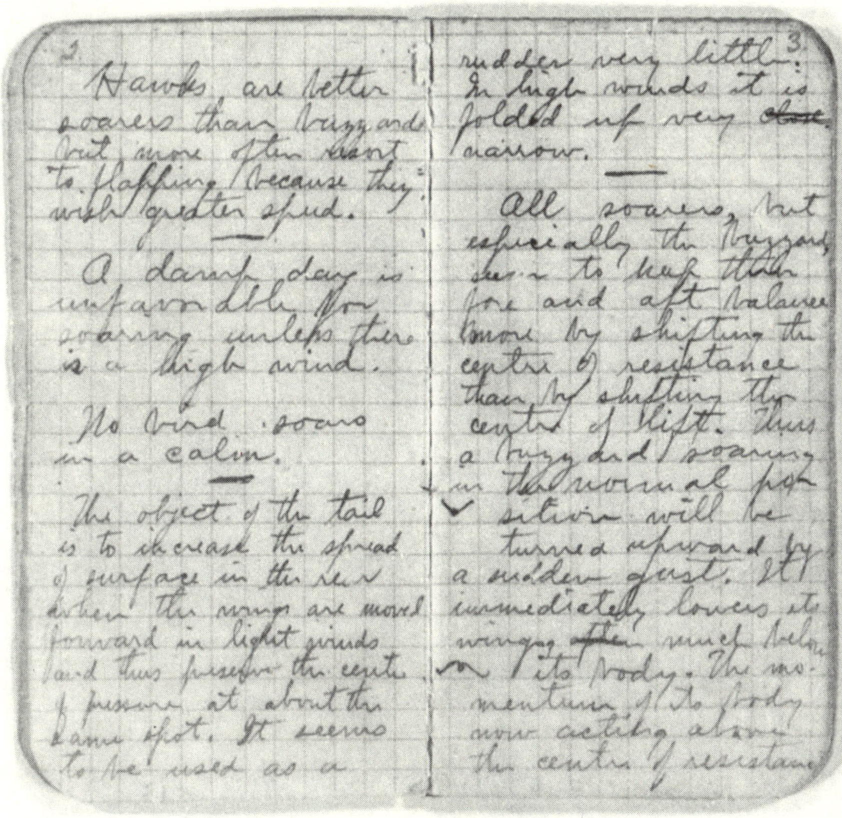

2.

Hawks are better soarers than buzzards but more often resort to flapping because they wish greater speed.

A damp day is unfavorable for soaring unless there is a high wind.

No bird soars in a calm.

The object of the tail is to increase the spread of surface in the rear when the wings are moved forward in light winds and thus preserve the centre of pressure at about the same spot. It seems to be used as a

3.

rudder very little. In high winds it is folded up very ~~close~~ narrow.

All soarers, but especially the buzzard, seem to keep their fore and aft balance more by shifting the centre of resistance than by shifting the centre of lift. Thus a buzzard soaring in the normal position will be turned upward by a sudden gust. It immediately lowers its wings ~~often~~ much below its body. The momentum of its body now acting above the centre of resistance

The wind and soaring birds made the banks a laboratory for flight (Kitty Hawk, 1900). *On their first trip to Kitty Hawk in 1900, Wilbur Wright thought he could discern the secrets of flight by observing the thousands of birds taking flight every day from the Carolina sounds. He sketched their majestic form while they soared over winds rising from the walls of sand dunes and over thermal plumes racing upward from sunbaked sands. He recorded his reflections in his diary at Kitty Hawk in 1900. Wilbur Wright Diary, 1900, 1–3 (Wilbur and Orville Wright Papers, Library of Congress).*

Hawks and buzzards thrived in the habitat of the sounds (Chocowinity Bay, ca. 1911). *North Carolina's state naturalist H. H. Brimley or one of his colleagues—perhaps the great female photographer Bayard Wootten—captured this scene of bird-nesting serenity, most likely on Chocowinity Bay in the upper reaches of Pamlico Sound near Washington, North Carolina. These birds may be among the flying creatures frequently described by the Wrights in their diaries. Photograph, perhaps Bayard Wootten, n.d. (PhC42 Bx5F31, Brimley Photograph Collection, State Archives of North Carolina, Raleigh).*

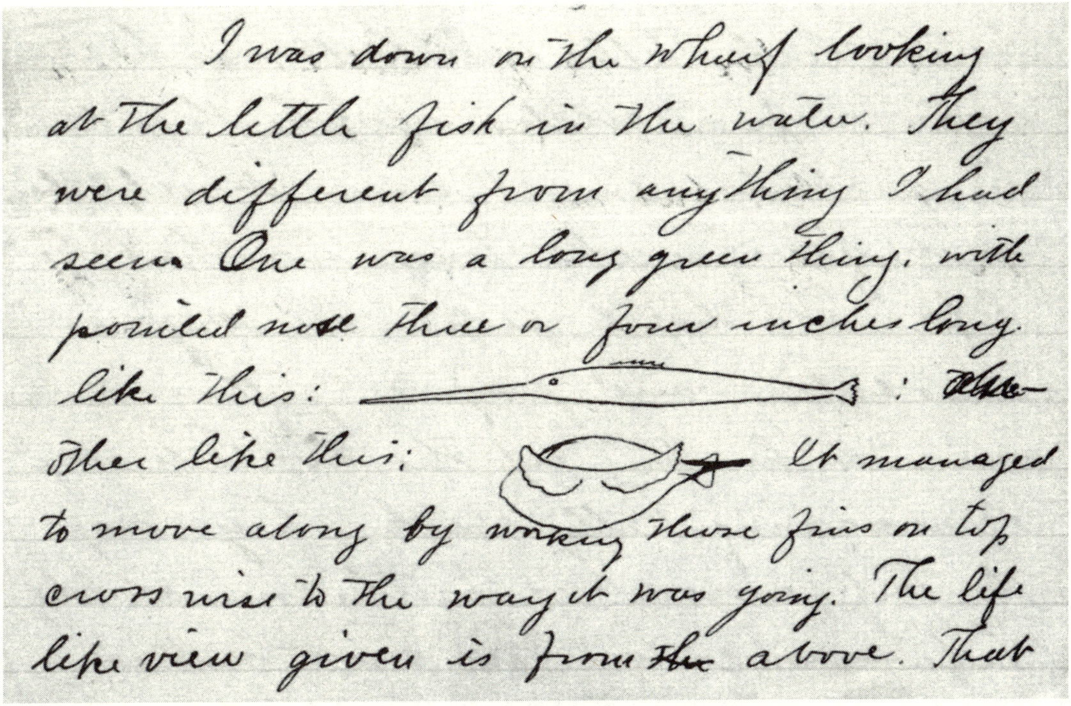

I was down on the wharf looking at the little fish in the water. They were different from anything I had seen. One was a long green thing, with pointed nose three or four inches long like this: : other like this: It managed to move along by working those fins on top cross wise to the way it was going. The life like view given is from above. That

Observations on fish propulsion in the Albemarle Sound (Elizabeth City, 1900). *Although Wilbur and Orville Wright were virtually conjoined partners in the invention of flight, Orville was always more interested in the mechanics of propulsion, including the manner in which fish advanced themselves through water. Orville was also interested in the various methods of catching fish for sport and for eating; he described them to his sister Katharine after his first visit in 1900 to the docks in Elizabeth City. Orville Wright to Katharine Wright, 28 September 1900 (Wilbur and Orville Wright Papers, Library of Congress).*

The banks were home to huddles of roaming cattle and wild ponies (near Hatteras, 1899). *Visitors to the Carolina banks around 1903 were fascinated by the roaming herds of unfenced cattle and wandering huddles of wild ponies that occupied many regions of the barrier islands. Neither bovines nor mammals from the horse family were indigenous to North America—having been introduced most likely by Spanish explorers in the sixteenth century. The man pictured is not identified. Photograph, Corydon Pirnie Cronk, 1899 (AV.5138, Carol Cronk Cole Collection, Outer Banks History Center, Manteo).*

Marauding swine knew no boundaries nor respected any encampment (Nags Head, ca. 1903). *The principal enemies of the Wright brothers and other visitors to the Carolina banks were mosquitoes, mice, and marauding pigs. Grunting and grubbing swine were the most incorrigible and persistent. To keep these intrepid creatures from their food supplies, the brothers used every weapon at their disposal—tent pegs, sling shots, and bloodcurdling screams to chase roaming pigs from their camps. Photograph, H. H. Brimley, ca. 1903 (PhC42 Bx1F1, Brimley Photograph Collection, State Archives of North Carolina, Raleigh).*

A forlorn victim of storms and salt-shear became a favorite natural landmark (Nags Head, ca. 1903). *The storm-bent tree, a seeming near-victim of hurricanes and nor'easters, became an iconic living landmark near the beach at Nags Head where residents and visitors alike wanted to have their picture made. For a time, at least in the early years of the twentieth century, the tree served as a symbol of the unique character of the banks region, with its brooding storms, windswept landscapes, surging waters, and other more enduring charms of nature. Photograph, forestry photographer, ca. 1903 (F3, State Agency Records, Forest Resources Group, Dare County, State Archives of North Carolina, Raleigh).*

2

NEGOTIATING NORTH CAROLINA'S INLAND SEA

When the Wright brothers made their way to Kitty Hawk, they each crossed the Albemarle Sound between Elizabeth City and Kitty Hawk at least a dozen times. In addition to making their own way across the sound, they provided information and guidance for their brother Lorin and for several other visiting aeronauts traveling from various places in the United States—some of them multiple times—on how to get from Elizabeth City to their campsite at Kill Devil Hills. They included Octave Chanute from Chicago; Augustus Herring from St. Joseph, Michigan; Edward Huffaker from Chunky City, Tennessee; and George Spratt from Coatesville, Pennsylvania. If the Wright brothers knew nothing about North Carolina's region of shallow sounds when they made their maiden voyage in 1900, they came to know it pretty well by the time of their fourth trip, when they undertook their first powered flight on 17 December 1903.

In 1900 Wilbur cursed his boat captain Israel Perry and his leaky *Curlicue* for presumed imbecilities in navigating his small sailboat across the sound. The name Israel Perry became an iconic term for a blundering idiot in the Wright family. When the brothers began to understand the complications of plying the waters of the sound, they had more respect—but little more patience—with Captain Franklin Harris Midgett (1860–1929). Beginning in 1902, Midgett operated a freight vessel—the *Lou Willis*, a sixty-foot, two-masted schooner—on a regular weekly or biweekly basis from his dock on the western edge of Kitty Hawk to and from Elizabeth City. The brothers faulted Midgett for operating on what they considered to be a sometimes irregular and unreliable basis. Yet they negotiated deals with him repeatedly to get their boxes of airplane parts, tools, and lumber from Elizabeth City to their camp at Kill Devil Hills. Despite their many complaints, they were always grateful when Midgett and his sons Truxton and Spencer hand-delivered the needed goods to their camp.[1]

By 1900 the sound region of North Carolina had become and was viewed by coastal geologists as an inland sea—somewhat akin to the Great Lakes of North America. It had developed a separate demography and system of commerce that made direct access to the Atlantic Ocean irrelevant. Some dreamed of somehow creating ports where there were none; other more pragmatic souls gravitated toward much more practical solutions. Given the fact that Mother Nature seemed to give and take inlets on a capricious and unpredictable basis, there were less costly and more reliable ways of making North Carolina's inland sea navigable—no matter the whims of climate. Just as the Wrights wanted to get their cargoes transported across the sound, hundreds of entrepreneurs and small-business operators in both North Carolina and Virginia dreamed of being able to exploit the rich resources of coastal Carolina potentially for great profits. There were fish, fruits, fowl, and forests in the Carolina firmament that could be used to fill the hungry maws and emerging industries of a blossoming nation. Every prospective producer, investor, businessman, and trader wanted to be able to get these precious—often perishable items—from source to table or factory in the most efficient manner possible.

George Washington (1732–99) and other big thinkers around the Chesapeake Bay region of Virginia had the right idea in the eighteenth century. As basically an architect and engineer at heart, Washington had dreamed before the American Revolution of building a canal that would drain the vast and tangled swamplands that lay partly in North Carolina and partly in Virginia. Such a canal would also create a reliable channel that would be impervious to the wiles of nature for moving goods—unprocessed or perishable—from North Carolina to the deep-water docks at Norfolk, Virginia. From the point of view of those same entrepreneurs, it would be possible to transport finished goods—cloth, tools, furniture, books, and distilled liquids—in the opposite direction to the thousands of hearty souls who lived around the banks region of North Carolina. This region had been viewed by explorers and colonial governors as an appendage to Virginia in any case. Thus it made sense for Virginia leaders and investors to work with Carolinians to create the necessary communication and transportation links to handle a potentially lucrative commerce.

Washington and his Virginia associates created the Dismal Swamp

Canal Company in 1793 to build this new spine of commerce. Despite the company's use of private funds and the employment of a small army of slaves, the first part of the canal was not opened for commerce until 1805. By 1810 it was reaping a handsome profit. The full canal, ranging from the Chesapeake Bay to the Albemarle Sound, opened for business in 1814—during the last phases of the War of 1812.[2] That time was propitious, for it coincided with both the closing of the Carolina inlets and the opening of one of America's greatest economic expansions following the War of 1812. The Dismal Swamp Canal—with a system of carefully engineered locks for raising and lowering cargo craft—worked very efficiently until the 1850s, when a rival canal following a far different route closer to sea level, the Albemarle and Chesapeake Canal, appeared.

Whereas the Dismal Swamp Canal had been built mainly by hand with slave labor, the Albemarle and Chesapeake was built between 1855 and 1859 with the aid of giant steam dredges that clawed away a wide ditch for the canal through the dense swamps that lay between Norfolk and the Albemarle Sound. Although the canal builders had to develop a unique locking system to balance the substantially different effects of lunar tides on the Chesapeake Bay (which is tidal) and the Albemarle Sound (nontidal), this majestic marvel of canal engineering opened on 9 January 1859. Its first customer was a brand-new iron barge—the *Enterprise*—with a full load-carrying capacity of six hundred bales of cotton or ten thousand bushels of grain.[3]

The state of North Carolina had expended millions of dollars during the early nineteenth century in a futile attempt to build a canal system that would connect its resident farmers and businesses to Carolina ports rather than to Virginia. But these two canals served North Carolina's inner coastal region just as effectively as the Erie Canal had linked Upstate New York to the port of New York City. The capacity of the Chesapeake Bay region to lure North Carolina business in the direction of Virginia was further exacerbated when a Norfolk-based company—the Norfolk Southern Railroad—opened a railroad line from Norfolk through Elizabeth City to Edenton in 1881. With the railroad came as well a fleet of shallow steamships that plied the Albemarle and Pamlico Sounds from that time forward, feeding both passengers and North Carolina's agricultural and forest products into the busy Norfolk Southern train stations.[4]

A separate company—the Norfolk, Virginia Beach and Southern—opened a second railroad line in 1898 that radiated from Norfolk as well and terminated at the head of Currituck Sound at the tiny village of Munden, Virginia. From a newly built wharf there, much closer to the fishing and fowling regions of Currituck, the company launched a second fleet of steamships that also crisscrossed the Albemarle Sound region, providing a separate highly competitive alternative for Carolina farmers, fishermen, and timber companies to access the rapidly expanding transport capacities of the Norfolk area.[5]

Just as expanded waterways were built in the second half of the nineteenth century, enabling large Canadian and American vessels to travel from Lake Superior across the Great Lakes and eventually into the large St. Lawrence River, the vastly upgraded Dismal and Albemarle and Chesapeake canals continued to carry cargo from North Carolina's inland sea to the Chesapeake transport hubs and northern markets well into the twentieth century. Despite the versatility of the railroads to compete with the canals in terms of both cost and efficiency, these old engines of the canal era survived and thrived. That was because the coastal Carolina region was an area that continued to be characterized principally by its waterways.

Indeed, by 1900 the region was already abuzz with the idea that the United States should create an inland waterway that could be traveled from Maine to Florida and, further, that the waterway should be built sufficiently inland that it could be traversed safely by both commercial vessels and pleasure craft. It was a new era for big canals—stimulated by the construction of the Suez Canal linking the Indian Ocean to the Mediterranean Sea and the building of the Panama Canal linking the Atlantic and the Pacific Oceans. What made the idea of an inland waterway all the more appealing to the people of coastal Carolina were the twin notions that it should be built totally at government expense and that it should be available from one end to the other free of charge. Tired of paying steep toll charges to commercial canals and the often discriminatory rate schemes of railroads, coastal Carolina farmers and fishermen joined other Americans in rebelling against business and transportation monopolies.

When North Carolina's Congressman John H. Small (1858–1946) from Washington, North Carolina, became a champion of an American inland waterway in Congress in 1899, he bespoke the wishes of coastal Carolinians. He got the U.S. Army Corps of Engineers to lay out a preferred route for the waterway from Norfolk to Beaufort, North Carolina, and secured federal government funding to begin work on that section of the national waterway in early 1908. For the first time in North Carolina history, the goal of making it possible for coastal craft large and small to bypass America's most dangerous wreck-strewn shore around Cape Hatteras through North Carolina's inland sea seemed achievable. Whether coastal inhabitants were in the business of harvesting fish, game, crops, or timber, they would be able to direct their trade, for the first time, either northward through Norfolk or southward through North Carolina's newly emerging ports at Beaufort and Morehead City. The Carolina coast was on the verge of opening the first link of America's water-based superhighway in the early years of the twentieth century.[6]

Thus, when the Wright brothers began traveling to North Carolina in 1900, there were no handy roadmaps from an automobile association that could be unfolded on the dining room table to chart a route of travel. In 1902 there were only 23,000 automobiles in the nation, compared with 17 million horses. And there were very few roads and routes that could be traversed by automobiles or that could easily be traveled for any distance by horse-drawn conveyances.[7] America in 1900 was a nation of trains and steamships that had been developed by high-stakes entrepreneurs and fiercely competitive companies—all with generous subsidies from both the national government and the states where they operated. Indeed, around 1900 the United States possessed the most efficient publicly available (though most links were privately owned) system of transportation it has ever enjoyed. The age of the private automobile and public roads had not yet begun—nor had, of course, anyone yet dreamed of an era of airports and air transportation.

Private railroad companies operated the spokes and hubs that made the system work. From Dayton, Ohio, the Wrights traveled by rail to Cincinnati (a major hub) where they had competitive options to get to Norfolk, Virginia. From Norfolk there were two spoke alternatives to take them to the Albemarle Sound—Elizabeth City or Mackeys in Currituck County; and from those two places the railroads operated steamships that crisscrossed the sounds to deliver passengers to (among other places) Manteo or Nags Head. The railroads and their steamships did not travel to Kitty Hawk (a tiny fishing village) or to Kill Devil Hills (no town existed). To get to those places one was on his or her own—as the Wright brothers (who were accustomed to train travel) learned.

When Wilbur left Dayton for Kitty Hawk on 11 September 1900, he therefore had confirmed rail-passenger tickets all the way to Elizabeth City by way of Norfolk: "Left Dayton Thurs. eve. at 6:30 p.m. over Big Four and C. & O. Arrived at Old Point [Comfort] about six o'clock p.m. the next day, and went over to Norfolk via the steamer *Pennsylvania*. Put up at the Monticello Hotel. . . . At 4:30 left for Eliz. City and put up at the Arlington where I spent several days waiting for a boat to Kitty Hawk."[8] But, beginning in 1901, and in the years after, the Wrights fabricated the components of their flying machines in Dayton and shipped huge boxes of freight—with tools, camp stoves, furnishings, and flying machines—

to Kitty Hawk. In 1901 and 1902 they organized their travel so that they would arrive simultaneously with their goods at Elizabeth City, from which they arranged private transport for themselves and their freight to Kitty Hawk. In 1903 they sent their freight ahead and booked themselves straight through to Manteo—going by steamship on the *Ocracoke* for the last public transportation leg from Elizabeth City to Manteo. From Manteo they traveled privately, by "gasoline launch," with their grocer, Theodore S. Meekins, to Kill Devil Hills.[9]

Much to their surprise, the Wright brothers eventually enjoyed a great deal of flexibility in reaching the Carolina coast and in shipping their flying machines there. That was because during the first thirty years following the Civil War, the northeastern corner of North Carolina had seen the development in their region of a comprehensive and highly efficient transportation system. One of those watching the changing scene was Frank Vaughan, an Elizabeth City attorney, who wrote an assessment of the transformation in 1895. He exclaimed that whereas in 1880 it had taken a minimum of thirteen hours to travel the fifty miles from his city to Norfolk at a cost of ten to fifteen dollars, by 1895 one could make the trip in an hour and a half for one to two dollars. And at Norfolk, one had the option of heading to Ohio (Wright territory) on either the Norfolk and Southern or the Chesapeake and Ohio railroads, or heading to Baltimore, Philadelphia, and New York either by one of two railroads or by one of two steamship lines—the Clyde Line of Philadelphia or the Old Dominion Steamship Company. And if one wanted to go south from Elizabeth City to the opposite end of the inland sea at Washington, North Carolina, or New Bern, one could go either by rail through Edenton and Roper or by Old Dominion Company steamships that traveled up the Roanoke and Chowan Rivers, as well as to a half dozen stops on the Pamlico River out of New Bern—not to mention Manteo on Roanoke Island and to the resort village of Nags Head on the banks.[10]

The increased speed at which people could travel was matched and exceeded by the remarkable number of options for moving product. Twenty-eight stations on the railroad lines going northward to Norfolk via Elizabeth City and thirty steamship landings around North Carolina's inland sea suddenly made it possible for the Carolina coastal region to become the food basket for the eastern metropolitan corridor of the United States. With an abundance of fish and fowl and fruits and vegetables available just for the harvesting, it became possible for the first time in North Carolina history for its farmers, fishermen, and hunters to commercialize the occupations they had been practicing for generations on end merely to supply their own tables. Whereas previously the principal commercial outputs from coastal Carolina had been forest products and cotton, virtually anything that could be grown, caught, or shot around the inland sea suddenly became a product with a ready means of getting it to market without spoilage.

All of this was possible because, with the revolutionary transportation system fully in place by 1900, perishable food products could be delivered to the cities of Washington, D.C., and Baltimore on the first morning after shipment. The same goods could be sold in Philadelphia and New York on the second morning and in Providence, Rhode Island, and Boston on the third morning. Fish, fruit, and birds of prey could be presented as fresh items and put on city tables straight from the source for the first time in North Carolina history. Fresh fish and oysters, corn and rice, tomatoes and cabbage, beans and melons suddenly became cash crops. North Carolina's almost inexhaustible supply of hardwoods, pulpwood, lumber, and specialty furniture woods also could be moved from forest to lumber processers, paper mills, and furniture factories scattered across the northeastern United States with an as-needed efficiency never known before.

No longer an American backwater by any meaning of the term, coastal Carolina, including the banks region, was finally by 1900 integrated economically into the fabric of a rapidly industrializing and urbanizing America. Its transportation system—the infrastructure of a booming nation—in the space of thirty years after the Civil War, had become fully state of the art. These were virtual boom times for the Carolina coast and its soil- and water-rich inland sea.

North Carolina's vast and navigable inland sea, 1890. *By the 1890s, North Carolina's upper sound region had become an inland sea bounded by a barrier island chain extending into the Atlantic Ocean on the east and by a mainland of numerous shallow rivers and streams on the west. It was mainly landlocked on every side, with only tiny inlet openings where rivulets of fresh water could flow into the ocean and tidal waves of salt water could mingle with the river-fed sounds. Detail of "Rand McNally and Co's New Map of North Carolina," 1890 (Cm912 1890r, North Carolina Maps, 617, North Carolina Collection, University of North Carolina at Chapel Hill).*

Shipping freight and people across the inland sea: The Midgetts (Kitty Hawk, ca. 1903). *Captain Franklin Harris Midgett (1860–1929) established a weekly or biweekly freight service between Elizabeth City and Kitty Hawk in 1902 and delivered the Wright brothers' 1902, 1903, and 1908 flying machines as well as building materials, groceries, and supplies to their camps at Kill Devil Hills. His son Truxton (1887–1978) (left) served as a courier between Kitty Hawk and Kill Devil Hills. Photograph, Norfolk Photographic Studio, ca. 1903 (Shirley D. Toler Private Collection, Havelock, North Carolina).*

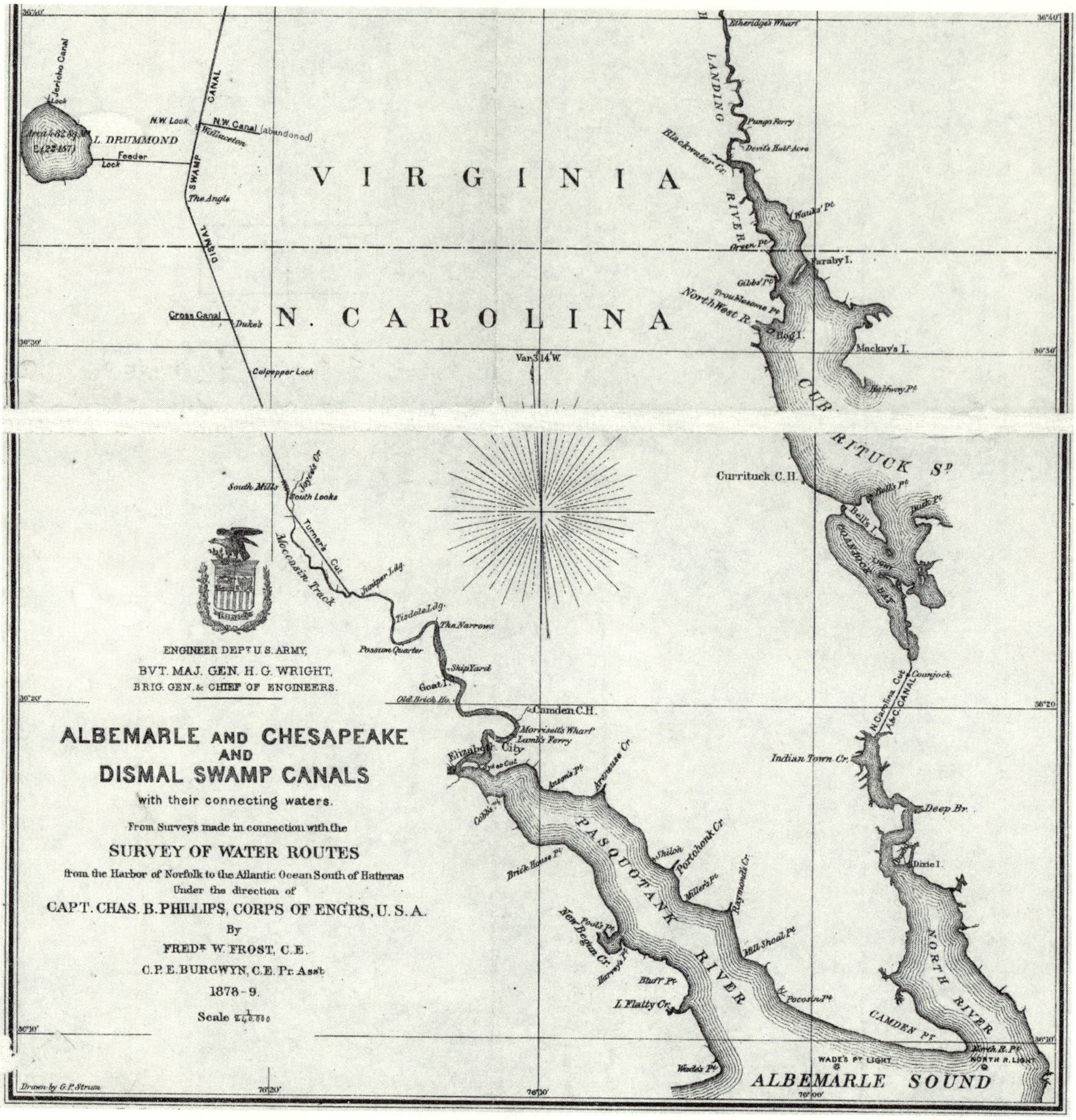

Two canals perpetuated the Albemarle region's links to Virginia. *When North Carolina's inlets closed in the early nineteenth century, the Dismal Swamp Canal—vigorously espoused by George Washington—became the Albemarle and Pamlico Sound region's principal outlet to the world. The addition of the shorter, wider, and deeper Albemarle and Chesapeake Canal in the 1850s expanded the historic connection of the Carolina coast to the Chesapeake Bay area of Virginia. Detail of U.S. Department of the Army, "Albemarle and Chesapeake and Dismal Swamp Canals," 1878–79 (Cm912.02 1879u1, North Carolina Maps, 878, North Carolina Collection, University of North Carolina at Chapel Hill).*

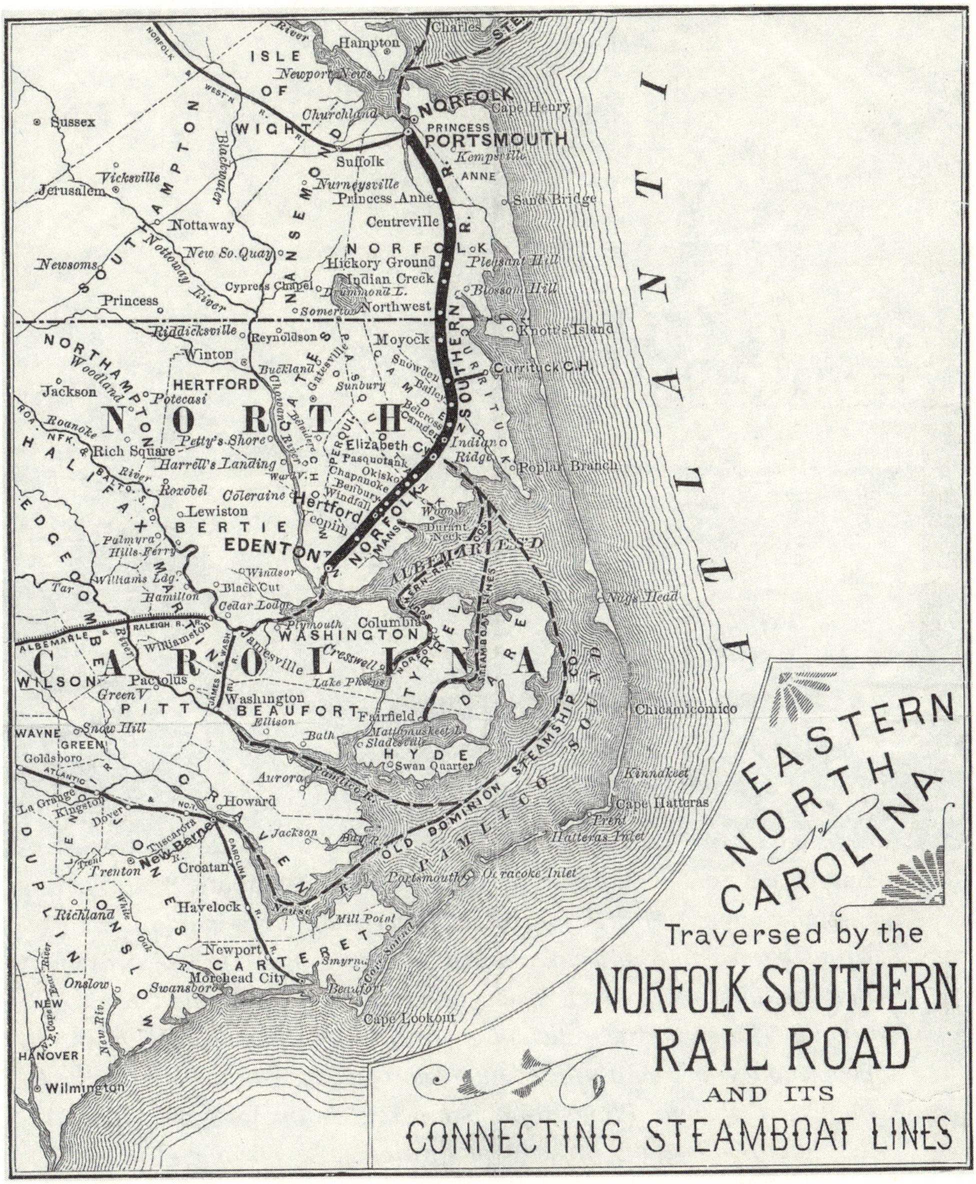

Railroads extended their coastal reach with steamboats. *The railroads begat steamboat lines that crisscrossed the sounds. Railroads crossed the Carolina sound region where there was firmament to lay crossties and rails to link coastal cities and towns to the outer world. The same companies pushed shallow-draft steamboats across the sounds connecting tiny towns to the national railroad spine. "Norfolk Southern Rail Road and Its Connecting Steamboat Lines," 1884 (Cm912.2 1884v, North Carolina Maps, 885, North Carolina Collection, University of North Carolina at Chapel Hill).*

Railroads sent a fleet of steamboats across the Albemarle Sound (sound region, ca. 1903). *The Norfolk and Southern Railway—in addition to its strings of passenger and cargo railcars—maintained a fleet of steamboats that spread the railway's tentacles across the Albemarle and Pamlico Sounds. This elaborate system of rail and water transport moved both people and goods across the sound region on a coordinated and reliable published schedule. Photograph, photographer unknown, ca. 1903 (PAS 242, Photo Collections, Museum of the Albemarle, Elizabeth City).*

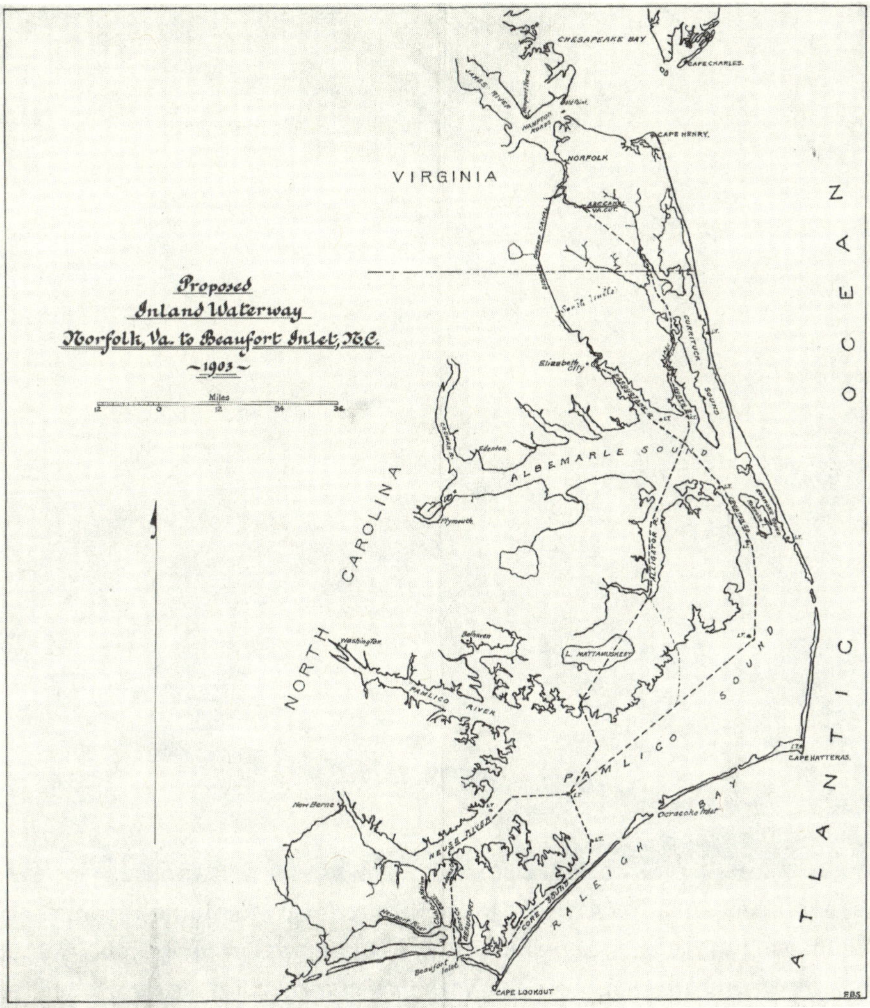

Coastal promoters envisioned a secure inland waterway. *By 1903 coastal Carolinians were promoting the construction of a great "Inland Waterway" inside North Carolina's dangerous barrier islands. Inspired by such complicated and acclaimed international passageways such as the Suez Canal, the Panama Canal, and the St. Lawrence Seaway, North Carolina congressman John H. Small secured funding for the U.S. Army Corps of Engineers to chart routes along either the Dismal Swamp or the Albemarle and Chesapeake Canals to Carolina's inland sea. U.S. Army Corps of Engineers, "Proposed Inland Waterway, Norfolk, Va. to Beaufort Inlet, N.C.," 1903 (Cm912.02 1903, North Carolina Maps, 877, North Carolina Collection, University of North Carolina at Chapel Hill).*

Taking the steamship *Ocracoke* from Elizabeth City to Manteo (sound region, ca. 1903). *On 23 September 1903, Wilbur and Orville Wright took the steamship* Ocracoke *on one of its regularly scheduled transits from Elizabeth City to Manteo. From there, they took a private gasoline launch to Kill Devil Hills, where, three months later, on 17 December, they conducted the world's first controlled, powered flight. Photograph, photographer unknown, ca. 1903 (PC.5099, Captain Henry Clark Bridgers Jr. Collection, Outer Banks History Center, Manteo).*

Every boat on the coast was also available for hire (Manteo, 1908). *Not only were regularly scheduled trains, public ferries, and mail boats available for travel around the Carolina coast; every fishing skiff around the inland sea not at the moment engaged in fishing was available for hire. The Wrights hired local fishermen to transport them from Manteo to Kill Devil Hills, and so did these newspaper reporters in May 1908 when they were assigned to get a scoop on and perhaps a photograph of the brothers' secret powered flights. Lantern slide, James Hare, 1908 (1501.623, James Hare Collection, Harry Ransom Research Center, University of Texas at Austin).*

Fish houses and docks occupied every slip of navigable water (sound region, ca. 1903). *In every nook and hamlet around the Carolina sounds, one encountered fishing boats, docks, and fish houses from which fishermen broadcast tons upon tons of fish harvested from both the freshwater Albemarle Sound and the briny waters of the Pamlico Sound for transshipment to ready markets. Photograph, photographer unknown, ca. 1903 (PhC42 Bx12F53, Brimley Photograph Collection, State Archives of North Carolina, Raleigh).*

Shipping fresh fish to market was a big business (probably Avoca, ca. 1903). *Harvesting and packaging fish for rapid shipment via steamboat and train up the eastern U.S. corridor was a major income-producing business around the Carolina sounds. The white and black workers in this photograph had just finished processing a large catch from adjacent waters and putting the fish in wooden cartons ready for transshipment. Photograph, photographer unknown, ca. 1903 (PhC42 Bx12F12, Brimley Photograph Collection, State Archives of North Carolina, Raleigh).*

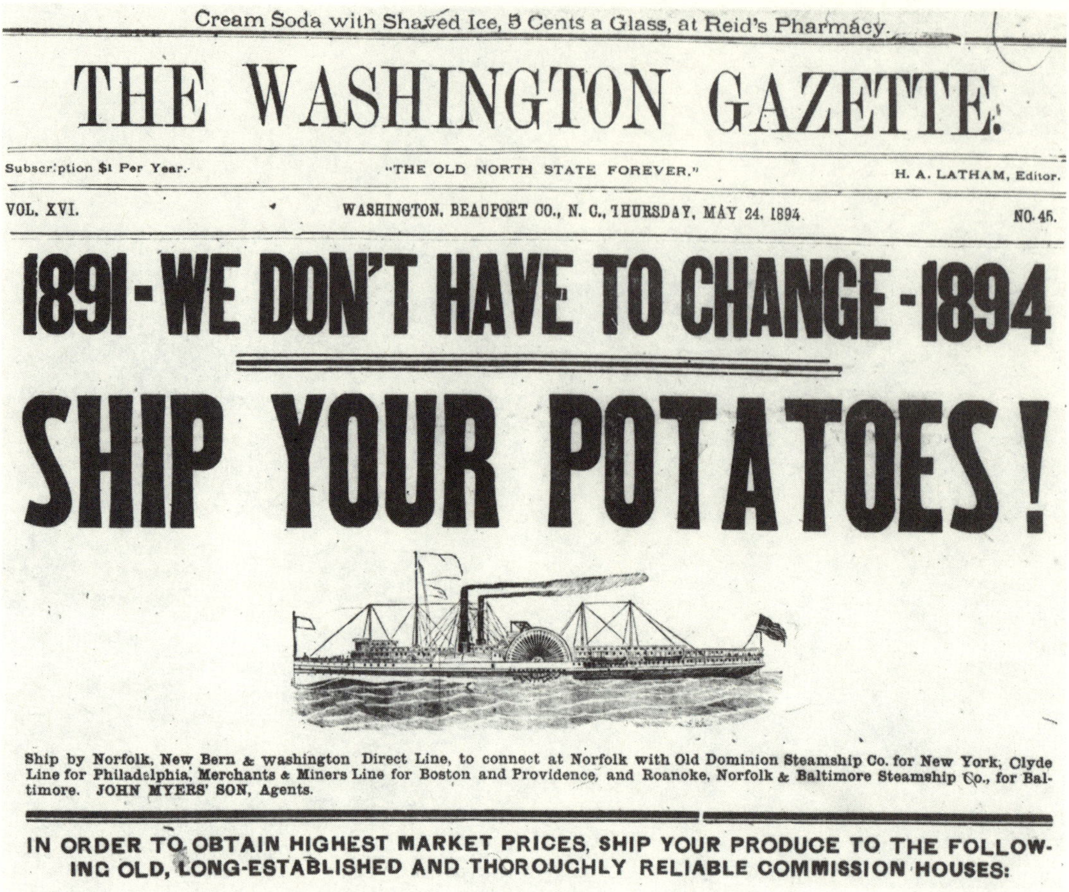

Cream Soda with Shaved Ice, 5 Cents a Glass, at Reid's Pharmacy.

THE WASHINGTON GAZETTE.

Subscription $1 Per Year. "THE OLD NORTH STATE FOREVER." H. A. LATHAM, Editor.

VOL. XVI. WASHINGTON, BEAUFORT CO., N. C., THURSDAY, MAY 24, 1894 NO. 45.

1891-WE DON'T HAVE TO CHANGE-1894

SHIP YOUR POTATOES!

Ship by Norfolk, New Bern & washington Direct Line, to connect at Norfolk with Old Dominion Steamship Co. for New York, Clyde Line for Philadelphia, Merchants & Miners Line for Boston and Providence, and Roanoke, Norfolk & Baltimore Steamship Co., for Baltimore. JOHN MYERS' SON, Agents.

IN ORDER TO OBTAIN HIGHEST MARKET PRICES, SHIP YOUR PRODUCE TO THE FOLLOWING OLD, LONG-ESTABLISHED AND THOROUGHLY RELIABLE COMMISSION HOUSES:

Steamboats and trains stood ready to race any product to market (advertisement, 1894). *No matter where one lived on the Carolina coast or in the sounds, or what one wanted to ship—fish, lumber, ducks, or potatoes—there were multiple steamships and railroads ready to provide the service. And they boldly advertised that they were prepared to carry products via express straight through to Baltimore, Philadelphia, New York, Providence, and Boston. Newspaper clipping,* Washington Gazette, *24 May 1894 (PC.5099, Captain Henry Clark Bridgers Jr. Collection, Outer Banks History Center, Manteo).*

Steamboats were available to rush reporters to Kill Devil Hills (Albemarle Sound, 1908). *A group of reporters from New York raced to the Carolina banks in May 1908 to get a headline scoop and perhaps a photograph of the Wright brothers' secret flights at Kill Devil Hills. Renowned photographer James Hare caught a staged glimpse of the competing journalists on their way from Elizabeth City to Manteo. Lantern slide, James Hare, 1908 (1498.620, James Hare Collection, Harry Ransom Research Center, University of Texas at Austin).*

Happy aeronauts also retreated leisurely from the Carolina coast (Manteo, 1911). *When the Wright brothers finished their experiments each year, whether satisfied or discouraged, they could depart from the Carolina coast in the same comfort and with the same reliability that had gotten them and the busy reporters there. In this picture Orville Wright (center)—rarely at ease with reporters—departed Manteo for Elizabeth City in 1911 comfortably chatting with four of the reporters who had been present during nearly all his ambitious soaring flights that year. By the last year of their experiments on the Carolina coast, the Wright brothers had learned that the Carolina transportation and communication infrastructure could satisfy their every need. Photograph, Van Ness Harwood, 1911 (805.1.f, Alpheus Drinkwater Collection, Joyner Library, East Carolina University, Greenville).*

3

CREATING A CLOCKWORK COAST

Unlike most people who have traveled to the banks of North Carolina since the late nineteenth century, neither Wilbur nor Orville Wright apparently ever visited any of the grand lighthouses that have graced the barrier islands since just after the American Civil War. They were so preoccupied with their mission to invent flight that they took few moments while at Kitty Hawk or Kill Devil Hills in the period from 1900 to 1903 to do the things tourists would normally have done either then or later. They saw the beams of light radiating across the ocean from both the Currituck and the Bodie Island Lighthouses, of course. But, in addition to the tall lighthouses facing the Atlantic Ocean to assist seagoing mariners, they also could not help noticing the many other lights around the inland sea behind the banks. In fact, on his first crossing of the Albemarle Sound in 1900, Wilbur remembered that his infamous skipper Israel Perry encountered one of the lights guiding sailors across the sounds. When Perry seemed to lose control of the *Curlicue*, Wilbur recalled, "there seemed nothing else to do but attempt to round the North River light and take refuge behind the point."[1]

During their visits to North Carolina the Wrights encountered a number of the "river lights" that were scattered at many critical points around the Albemarle Sound. Indeed, at the turn of the twentieth century, as many as twenty such lights enabled mariners to find the mouths of rivers pouring into the sounds—the North, Pasquotank, Chowan, Alligator, Roanoke, Pamlico, and Neuse. Others guided mariners through the shallow narrows of the much smaller passageways known as the Currituck, Croatan, and Roanoke Sounds. Still others helped them avoid reefs and shoals scattered almost everywhere around the sounds (Long, Gull, Bluff, Point Royal, the Brant Island Shoals, and Oliver Reef). Taken together these lights converted the shallow sounds into a navigable body of water, where—except during daylight hours or in heavy fog—a mariner could see beacons of light near every passage and on top of every major hazard. When fog settled on these waters, each of the local navigation lights also had an impressive bell to clang out the location of these hazards.

The business of lighting the Carolina coast and its inland sea was a huge operation by the opening of the twentieth century, involving five gigantic lighthouses facing the ocean between the Virginia border on the north and Cape Lookout at the southern tip of the barrier island chain. The shortest (65 feet) and the oldest (1823) of the lights was the Ocracoke Light, located on the island and inlet of that name. The other lights were much taller and all either newly built or rehabilitated between 1859 and 1875: Cape Hatteras (198.49 feet); Cape Lookout (169 feet); Bodie Island (161 feet); and Currituck Beach (161 feet). These impressively large lights—all with individualized black-and-white color schemes and distinctive light signals—were intended to send out beams of light to make it possible for mariners to see at least one blinking light—whether for navigation or for warning—from any ocean vantage point outside of the hazardous Carolina banks.[2]

Although there had been lighthouses on the coast of North Carolina from the 1790s forward—mainly at the most dangerous points for mariners (Cape Hatteras and Cape Lookout and at the port entry at Ocracoke), the building and maintenance of lighthouse beacons for seagoing mariners became the most important function of the U.S. Lighthouse Board, established in 1851. Under the watchful eye of the board, a new wave of eighty- to ninety-foot brick structures appeared along the U.S. coast during the 1850s—many of them to be prized tactical properties for both the Confederate and Union governments during the Civil War. The disputed and damaged lights of the Civil War era were replaced in the 1870s by the magnificent brick towers that were on the Carolina coast in 1900 and have been there ever since.[3]

It was also the responsibility of the federal Lighthouse Board, working with the U.S. Army Corps of Engineers, to light the canals, rivers, and shoals of North Carolina's inland sea. The board oversaw the lighting of entry points to the Dismal Swamp Canal and the Albemarle and Chesapeake Canal. By the time the Albemarle and Chesapeake Canal opened in 1859, "river lights" (squatty lighthouses that were actually houses built on cast-iron pilings) operated at Pamlico Point (1828), Roanoke Marshes (1831), and Croatan Shoal (1835). The lights at Bogue Banks, Hatteras

Beacon, and Wade's Point were opened in 1855, followed by another at Northwest Point Royal Shoal in 1857. Following the Civil War, when federal patrol boats plied these waters and a new era of commerce began, additional lights were quickly built at the entrances to the Neuse, North, and Roanoke Rivers (1862–66). Other obstructions in the sounds were systematically marked with still more lights in 1867 at Brant Island, Harbor Island Bar, Long Shoal, and Southwest Royal Point Shoal. Along with a few further river lights added later, by 1900 there was a network of river lights at every critical juncture in the sounds.[4]

Tall lighthouses on the ocean side of the Carolina banks and river lights across the Albemarle and Pamlico Sounds not only provided a navigational and transportation infrastructure to coastal Carolina; they also added important elements to the economic and social fabric of the complicated watery region. Every lighthouse required a keeper who lived at or even inside the lighthouse structure—as was also the case for each of the river lights. The keepers of these visible reminders of a federal government presence in the area became some of the most identifiable individuals in the most remote weather-beaten area of the state. They were federal government employees and pensioners. They wore militarylike uniforms. Their families got free housing at the lighthouse or on the river light. With access to weather data and government channels of communication, they were the earliest members of a national emergency force that would eventually become the U.S. Coast Guard in the twentieth century and Homeland Security in the twenty-first.

Lighthouse keepers were on duty virtually around the clock every day of the year; they were the caretakers and managers of America's most visible symbols of a nation making a place for itself in the world of commerce and military capabilities. Their responsibilities both as physical custodians of the lights and as symbols of authority were such that in 1902 the U.S. Lighthouse Board published a definitive manual titled *Instructions to Light-Keepers and Masters of Light-House Vessels*. Each keeper in its national system of navigational lights was expected to know the manual by heart and to adhere to it uniformly. The manual detailed all facets of the keeper's life: matters of dress, demeanor, and community engagement, as well as technical information on keeping daily journals, keeping lights in well-oiled operating condition, and constantly repairing and painting the lighthouse facilities.[5]

It is thus little wonder that most visitors from the mainland—aside from the Wright brothers—and travelers from distant lands found the lighthouses and river lights along North Carolina's coast around 1900 as among the most intriguing places to see and visit. The lighthouses were visible landmarks rising like giants above the virtually flat coastal plain. Both professional photographers and an increasing number of amateurs learning the art of exposing glass plates in a bulky bellows camera found lighthouse structures worthy of being photographed; they were places to take pictures of impressive lighthouse keepers and their families and sites where local residents could gather to snap a family photograph that would remind their children and grandchildren of life on the Carolina banks around the time that the Wright brothers flew their first powered airplane.

But if Wilbur and Orville Wright took little interest in luxuriating in the shadow of lighthouses during their six journeys to the coast of North Carolina, they became intimately acquainted with another group of installations also built and maintained by the U.S. government along the Carolina coast—lifesaving stations and the crews that manned them. They especially came to know the stations and their resident surfmen at Kitty Hawk and Kill Devil Hills.

New to the ways of beachside existence, the Wrights depended on the carefully designed and well-equipped stations and their mainly home-grown crews for a variety of important services: access to native know-how; connections to the outside world; and especially by 1903, vital lifting and toting assistance as the brothers' inventions progressed from light and nimble gliders to heavy motor-powered flying machines. In addition to being their only neighbors during extended sojourns on the coast, the seasoned characters who made up the crews of the lifesaving stations also introduced the Wrights to a water- and wind-oriented culture that indelibly influenced the brothers' outlook on how and when to challenge the constantly changing conditions of nature and climate.

The brothers were, in fact, introduced to the unusual coastal weather conditions by Joseph J. Dosher, the keeper of the U.S. Weather Station at Kitty Hawk (located adjacent to the Kitty Hawk Life-Saving Station). In a letter of 16 August 1900, Dosher—who became the brothers' most reliable adviser on the constantly changing weather—revealed that "the wind flows mostly from the North and Northeast." Since the sixty-mile barrier island was "about one mile wide clear of trees or high hills," the brothers could conduct test flights along "many miles of steady wind with a free sweep."[6] Between 1900 and 1903, Dosher provided the brothers with accurate information on weather conditions at the Kitty Hawk station. And so did the men at the Kitty Hawk Life-Saving Station, which had been established in 1874. Standing side by side on the beach at Kitty Hawk, these two U.S. government facilities afforded the Wrights both information on current atmospheric conditions and generations of weather savvy through the locally recruited men who staffed them.

When the brothers moved their flight operations permanently in 1901 to the lofty sand dunes at Kill Devil Hills four miles south of Kitty Hawk, they formed a new bond with the crew at the Kill Devil Hills Life-Saving Station. These men would become their first ground crew for handling their flying machines, as well as trustworthy witnesses to attest that the brothers did indeed perform the world's first man-controlled powered flight. Fortunately for the history of the beginnings of flight, the brothers used their photographic skills to take an indelible picture of their first powered flight (snapped by a lifesaver). But, in the process, they also recorded revealing images of the North Carolina lifesavers and their special world. Fascinated by the rough-hewn character of the lifesavers, the Wrights established a friendship and dependence on the Kitty Hawk and Kill Devil Hills lifesavers that continued for many years beyond their trips to North Carolina.

The presence of the national government on the Carolina coast was abundantly evident through the complex system of lifesaving stations that by 1900 populated the Carolina coast from Virginia to South Carolina. By 1900 there were lifesaving stations—each with a crew of at least seven men (six crew members and a station keeper)—located at intervals of approximately every seven miles from Cape Henry near the Virginia border to Cape Lookout—the most hazardous sections of the Carolina coast. Although lifesaving crews were drawn from local families across the river sounds, their focus—like that of the keepers of the tall lighthouses—was to make the Atlantic Ocean a safer place for the navigation of sailing ships and newer fleets of steam-driven craft that hugged the American coast carrying cargoes and people between small ports from the coast of northern Maine to the southern tip of Florida.[7]

The saving of lives from distressed ships was a function of the national government that arose slowly during the 1840s and 1850s following a surge of shipwrecks that involved the loss of scores of passengers, including families and children. Although once viewed as the responsibility of volunteers, a new U.S. Life-Saving Service was formed in the 1870s when a new cadre of journalists and sketch artists began dramatizing in word and image the destruction of ships in hurricane-force winds and raging seas. Winslow Homer, Thomas Nast, Howard Pyle, and Milton J. Burns—illustrators as well as fine artists—filled the pages of the illustrated *Harper's Weekly*, *Scribner's Monthly*, and *Frank Leslie's Newspaper* with gripping images of seaborne human tragedies. Other illustrations depicted deaths averted through the heroic efforts of nearly anonymous lifesavers.[8]

The events that forced Congress to formally create and greatly expand the U.S. Life-Saving Service in 1878 were two well-publicized, back-to-back ship crashes on the Carolina coast. The U.S. Navy's wooden warship *Huron* ran aground just north of the lifesaving station at Nags Head in November 1877. The steamship *Metropolis* foundered in the shadow of the Currituck Beach Lighthouse at Corolla, North Carolina, just two months later, in January 1878. Through the efforts of the lifesavers at Nags Head, two dozen members of the crew of 132 sailors on the *Huron* were saved. Despite the heroic efforts of residents, visiting hunters, and lifesavers from the Kitty Hawk Life-Saving Station, 85 of the 250 passengers—mainly laborers bound for Brazil—perished in the sinking of the *Metropolis*.[9]

The concentration of illustrated magazines on the human travails of shipwrecks aside, there was also the loss of cargo and the ships themselves. Merchant vessels operated by upright businessmen carried maritime insurance that had to be adjusted in the case of an unforeseen disaster. Whereas longtime banks residents had worn a well-deserved reputation for salvaging and guarding treasures that washed ashore from sunken ships, shipowners and their insurance companies welcomed the creation of the U.S. Life-Saving Service not only for saving lives but also for providing an onsite orderly service for protecting both salvaged cargoes and ships that could perhaps be refloated.

From 1878 onward, a full force of nearly two dozen lifesaving stations on the Carolina coast dealt with the contrary destructive forces of both nor'easters and hurricanes when they lashed the banks and forced the abandonment of ships hugging too closely to the shore. When a giant storm in 1879 opened two new inlets and leveled towns on the lower banks, lifesavers were at the ready to help out. But this storm was minor compared with the most destructive hurricanes on record, which occurred in the summer and fall of 1899—just before the Wrights made their first trip to the banks. The Great Hurricane of 1899 known as San Ciriaco (because of its destructive path through Puerto Rico) wreaked havoc across the length and breadth of the banks in August that year. Nags Head suffered a direct hit. At least a dozen ships sank along the coast or were lost forever at sea. This was followed by a second hurricane in October that pummeled the Cape Fear region of North Carolina, uprooting trees and leveling houses on the backside of the Carolina sounds.[10]

San Ciriaco had a permanent effect on the psyche of the residents of the Carolina coast. It was one of the first hurricanes to acquire a permanent name (by happenstance, of course). Coming as it did at the opening of a new century, this massively destructive storm inspired the U.S. Weather Bureau to begin charting the track of every hurricane-force storm from that time forward. But it was also the first major storm following the full advent of photography. Corydon Pirnie Cronk, keeper of the U.S. Weather Station at Cape Henry, Virginia, made a voyage down the Carolina coast in 1899 to chart the immediate effects of the storm. And the Wright brothers followed just twelve months later, making their own photographic record of the Carolina coast during the first year of its recovery from the great storms of 1899. Finally, with the aid of photography, we had the benefit of seeing immediate time-scaled images of the destructive havoc of those hurricanes that crossed Caribbean islands and hugged the Atlantic coastline every year between August and October.

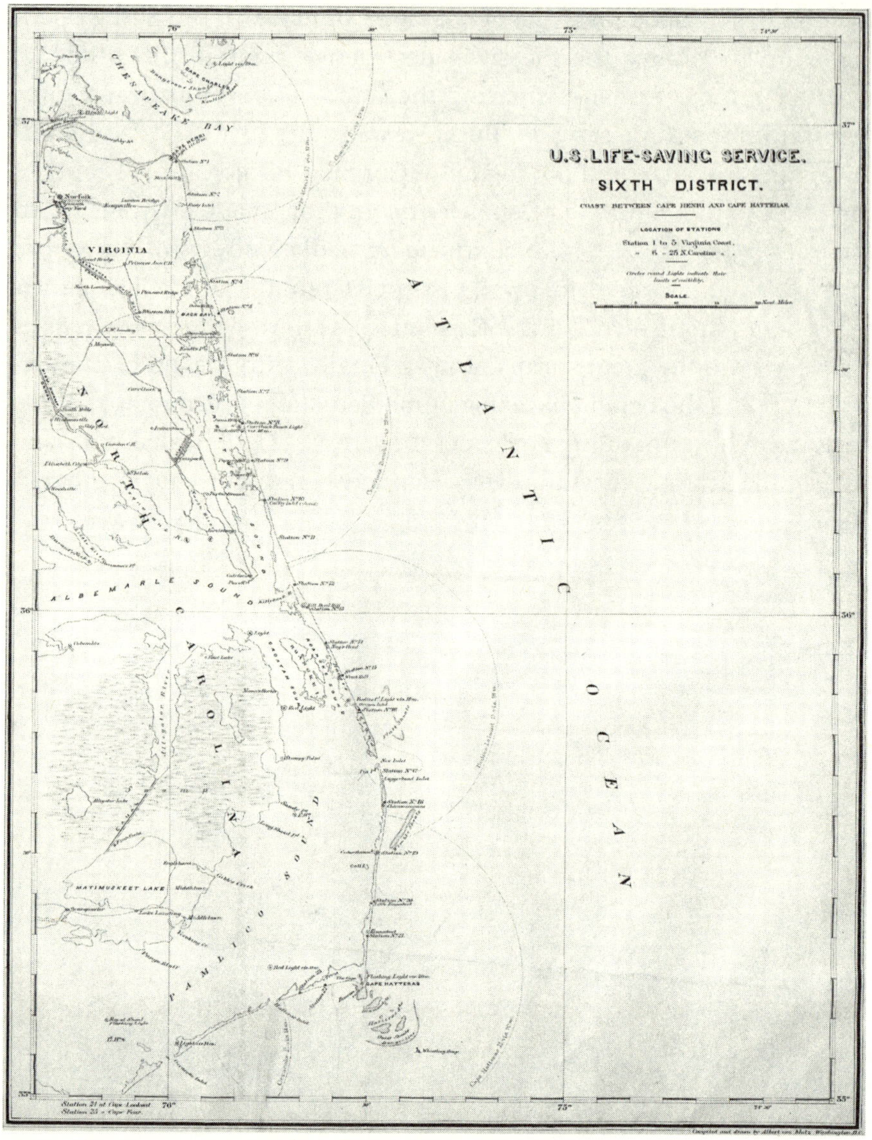

Illuminating and protecting North Carolina's dangerous coast, ca. 1900. *The upper banks region of North Carolina was one of the most dangerous coastlines in North America. It thus required the deployment of the most plentiful array of lighthouses and lifesaving stations in the nation. This map of the sixth district of the U.S. Life-Saving Service graphically portrays the intermingling of lighthouses and lifesaving stations along the Carolina coast. U.S. Life-Saving Service, "Sixth District Coast between Cape Henry and Cape Hatteras," ca. 1900 (Twiddy and Company, Corolla, North Carolina).*

The Currituck Beach Lighthouse installation (Corolla, ca. 1903).
The Currituck Beach Lighthouse—like the other tall lights on the Carolina coast—was actually a complex of U.S. government buildings that supported the light's operation. Prior to an era of electricity and automation, the gas lamps of the tall lights required operational attention around the clock and facility maintenance throughout the year. While North Carolina's other tall lights displayed unique black-and-white geometric patterns painted on their solid brick walls, the Currituck lighthouse was never painted, always bearing a simple brick face. Photograph, photographer unknown, n.d. (AV.5125.75-39011, H. H. Bamber Collection, Outer Banks History Center, Manteo).

Lighthouse complexes were often remote family homes (Corolla, ca. 1903). *Real people with complicated lives operated and took care of North Carolina's tall lighthouses. They procreated and lived at the lighthouses with their families in remote locations—often bereft of schools, physicians, or other social and cultural amenities. The lightkeeper's residence at Currituck Beach Lighthouse, shown here, was designed for simultaneous occupation by two growing families. Photograph, photographer unknown, n.d. (AV.5125.75-39011, detail, H. H. Bamber Collection, Outer Banks History Center, Manteo).*

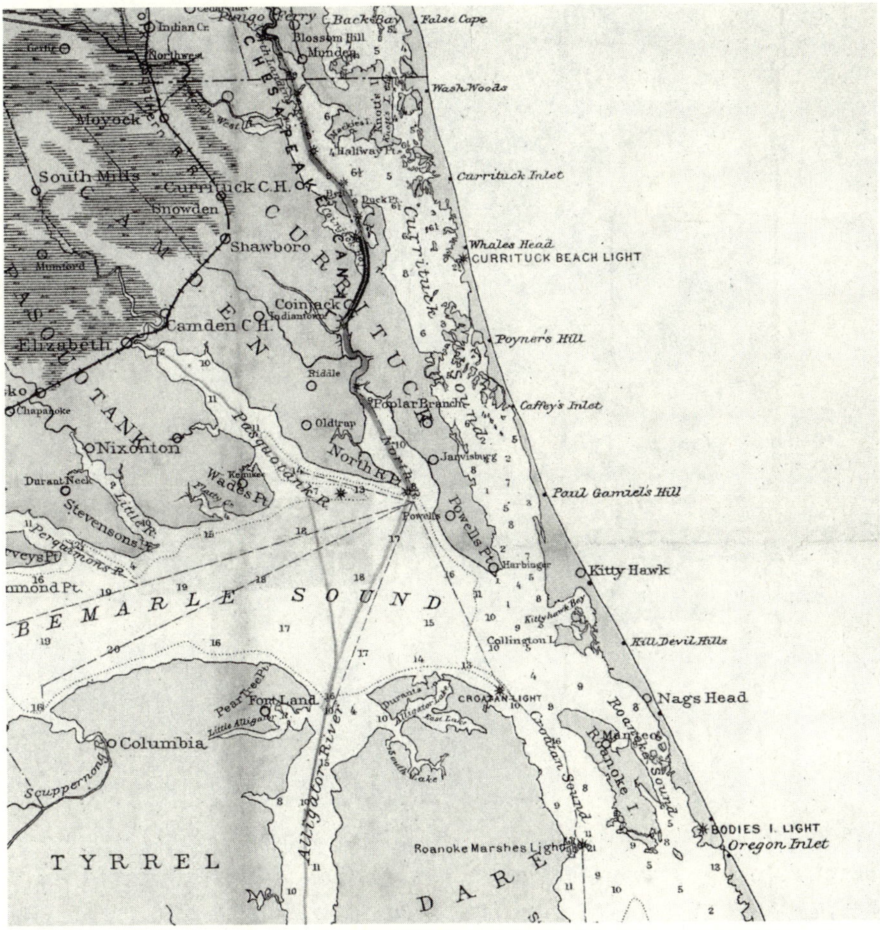

River lights outnumbered lighthouses in North Carolina (Albemarle Sound, 1902). *In addition to tall lighthouses, as at Currituck Beach, the U.S. Lighthouse Board also maintained a much larger network of "river lights" around North Carolina's complicated estuary and sound regions. The locations of these lights inside the banks are indicated by asterisks on the map. River lights were located at the entrances to the Pasquotank and North Rivers (upper right); along the route of the Albemarle and Chesapeake Canal's link to a second canal bisecting the Currituck Peninsula by the canal town of Coinjock; and at the northern and southern entrances to the Croatan Sound. Detail of U.S. Coast Survey, "Map of the Albemarle and Chesapeake Canal," 1902 (Cm912.02 1885L, North Carolina Maps, 884, North Carolina Collection, University of North Carolina at Chapel Hill).*

Wade Point River Light at the mouth of the Pasquotank River (Wade Point, ca. 1903). *The Wade Point River Light guided vessels into and out of the port of Elizabeth City. Some river lights were inhabited (such as Wade Point), and others served as unmanned navigation markers. Like the coastal lighthouses, the river lights in houses built atop cast-iron pilings and frames were inhabited by keepers and their families with round-the-clock duties. Photograph, photographer unknown, ca. 1903 (AV.5169, River Lights of North Carolina Collection, Outer Banks History Center, Manteo).*

The imposing Roanoke River Light, ca. 1903. *The Roanoke River Light was bulkier and taller than the Wade Point Light. Its characteristic bell was placed atop an observation tower adjacent to a much more spacious second or half floor. It stood at the mouth of the Roanoke River between the small river town of Plymouth and the historic Albemarle Sound crossing at Mackey's Ferry. Photograph, photographer unknown, ca. 1903 (AV.5169.3-7-1914, River Lights of North Carolina Collection, Outer Banks History Center, Manteo).*

The *Diamond Shoals Lightship* aground at Cape Hatteras, 1899. *The U.S. Lighthouse Board for decades attempted to maintain a stationery lighthouse on top of the dangerous Diamond Shoals several miles beyond the Cape Hatteras Lighthouse in the Atlantic Ocean. But every structure was soon destroyed. To solve the problem, Congress authorized the construction of a floating light, the* Diamond Shoals Lightship, *at the site in 1897. Despite its mobility in the face of storms, the* Diamond Shoals *was driven ashore during the San Ciriaco hurricane of 1899. Photograph, Corydon Pirnie Cronk, 1899 (AV.5138, Carol Cronk Cole Collection, Outer Banks History Center, Manteo).*

The lighthouse tender *Maple* (Albemarle Sound, ca. 1903). *The task of building and maintaining five tall lighthouses, two dozen river lights, and scores of unmanned buoy lights—not to mention a bobbling lightship—across the Carolina coast and its inland sea was a large and expensive business. The U.S. Lighthouse Board thus maintained a separate fleet of tender ships with a small army of workers to care for both the lights and the structures that supported them. The lighthouse tender* Maple *was kept busy on the Carolina coast racing from one light to another with fuel, lenses, wicks, replacement parts, tools, and vital communications among the small cadre of professional lighthouse keepers. Photograph, photographer unknown, ca. 1903 (PC.5099, Captain Henry Clark Bridgers Jr. Collection, Outer Banks History Center, Manteo).*

The Bodie Island Lighthouse complex (Bodie Island, 1899). *The lighthouse, with its distinctive pattern of black-and-white perimeter circles was just as remotely positioned as its architectural twin at Currituck Beach. In this photograph taken by meteorologist Corydon Pirnie Cronk just weeks after the San Ciriaco hurricane had passed across the Carolina coast in August 1899, it is clear that the light and its adjacent buildings had well-survived the destructive path of the storm. Photograph, Corydon Pirnie Cronk, 1899 (AV.5138, Carol Cronk Cole Collection, Outer Banks History Center, Manteo).*

The crew at the Kitty Hawk Life-Saving Station in 1900 (Kitty Hawk, 1900). *This crisp close-up of the Kitty Hawk lifesavers taken by Orville Wright drew a vivid picture of the station's crew on a typical day. Although the U.S. Life-Saving Service was a quasi-military organization (precursor to the U.S. Coast Guard), the informality of their uniforms was evident in this photograph. The men, recruited nearby, plied the local waters as fishermen or boatmen when not on duty. Left to right: Robert Lee Griggs, Robert Fulton Sanderlin, Thomas Edward Hines, Joseph Edward Baum (cook), Captain Samuel J. Payne, James Riley Best, and Thomas Nelson Sanderlin. Glass plate negative, Orville Wright, 1900 (L551, Wright Brothers Collection, Library of Congress). (See also Larry E. Tise,* Hidden Images: Discovering Details in the Wright Brothers' Kitty Hawk Photographs, 1900–1911 *[Charleston: History Press, 2005], 32–35.)*

The Kitty Hawk Weather Station (Kitty Hawk, 1899). *In 1899 the U.S. Weather Bureau photographer Corydon Pirnie Cronk took a close-up image of the Kitty Hawk Weather Station with its exterior stairway to its own crow's nest on the building's roof and to the station's array of weather-measuring devices. In addition to transmitting daily information onto a national information grid of weather data, the station's onsite meteorologist, Joseph J. Dosher, provided the Wright brothers with up-to-date weather conditions and transmitted occasional messages for them on the station's telegraph system—including a message to their family on 17 December 1903 reporting their first successful powered flight. Photograph, Corydon Pirnie Cronk, 1899 (AV.5138, Carol Cronk Cole Collection, Outer Banks History Center, Manteo).*

The crew at the Kill Devil Hills Life-Saving Station (Kill Devil Hill, 1902). *Lorin Wright probably took this exquisite photograph of the Kill Devil Hills Station and its crew while visiting his brothers' camp in October 1902. This image, showing the crew in their white fair-weather uniforms, reveals the simplicity of the station, as do the open window and the broken windowpane on its dormitory level. From left to right: William Thomas Beacham (probably), John T. Daniels (photographer of the first powered flight), "Uncle" Bennie O'Neal, and Adam T. Etheridge (caretaker for the Wrights' buildings). Glass plate negative, Lorin Wright, 1902 (L600, Wright Brothers Collection, Library of Congress). (See also Tise,* Hidden Images, *68–69.)*

Foundered wreck of the *E. S. Newman* from 1896 (Pea Island, 1899). *In addition to rescuing passengers from foundering or sinking ships, the U.S. Life-Saving Service was also responsible for overseeing the protection and disposition of shipwrecks and their cargoes—as in the case of the schooner* E. S. Newman *that ran aground near the Pea Island Life-Saving Station in October 1896. Photograph, Corydon Pirnie Cronk, 1899 (AV.5138, Carol Cronk Cole Collection, Outer Banks History Center, Manteo).*

Wreckage of the barkentine *Priscilla* in September 1899 (Gull Shoal, 1899). *The* Priscilla, *headed toward Cape Hatteras, ran aground between the Gull Shoal and Little Kinnakeet Life-Saving Stations at 10 p.m. on the night of 17 August 1899. In the thrashing waves of the storm, it broke into two pieces. Before Surfman Rasmus S. Midgett came on the scene, the wife of the ship's captain, two of his sons, and a cabin boy had already washed overboard and perished. Photographer Corydon Cronk took this picture of lifesavers and curious local residents one month after the tragic incident. Photograph, Corydon Pirnie Cronk, 1899 (AV.5138, Carol Cronk Cole Collection, Outer Banks History Center, Manteo).*

The enormous spillage of cargo from the barkentine *Priscilla* (Gull Shoal, 1899). *In the deep darkness on the night of 17 August 1899, Surfman Rasmus S. Midgett from the Gull Shoal Station "discovered buckets, barrels, boxes, and other articles coming ashore, which satisfied him that there was a wreck somewhere in the neighborhood." Two miles farther down the beach, he could hear "the outcries of shipwrecked men" (Life-Saving Service Annual Report, 1899). The photographer Corydon Cronk captured this image of the same scattered cargo from the* Priscilla *one month later. Photograph, Corydon Pirnie Cronk, 1899 (AV.5138, Carol Cronk Cole Collection, Outer Banks History Center, Manteo).*

Public auction of salvaged cargo and goods from the *Priscilla*, 1899. *In addition to saving the passengers of ships, the U.S. Life-Saving Service prepared incident reports on shipwrecks and assisted in the salvaging of both ships and their cargo. Owners, investors, and insurers were then able to conclude a financial settlement—including the sale of any cargo, tools, or equipment salvaged from the wreck. In September 1899—only a month after the San Ciriaco hurricane and a dizzying number of shipwrecks on the banks between Oregon Inlet and Cape Hatteras—insurance adjusters and local officials arranged a public auction to dispose of salvaged goods from the foundered vessels. The photographer Corydon Cronk was present at Gull Shoal to take this picture when residents of the banks congregated on their shad boats to inspect wreckage from the* Priscilla *and to place their bids for salvaged items. Photograph, Corydon Pirnie Cronk, 1899 (AV.5138, Carol Cronk Cole Collection, Outer Banks History Center, Manteo).*

Heroes of Gull Shoal Station in the San Ciriaco storm of 1899 (Gull Shoal, ca. 1903). *Surfman Rasmus S. Midgett of the Gull Shoal Station (built 1878) almost single-handedly saved ten members of the crew of the barkentine* Priscilla *when it ran aground on the night of 17 August 1899 in the San Ciriaco hurricane. Midgett encountered the wreck while on routine patrol south of his station. For his swift and heroic actions in rescuing the surviving victims individually and delivering them to safety, he was awarded the rare Gold Lifesaving Medal of Honor one month later (See Joe A. Mobley,* Ship Ashore! The U.S. Lifesavers of Coastal North Carolina *[Raleigh: North Carolina Division of Archives and History, 1994], 125–27). Photograph, photographer unknown, ca. 1903 (N.77.4.27, Brimley Photograph Collection, State Archives of North Carolina, Raleigh).*

Heroes of Little Kinnakeet Station in the San Ciriaco storm (Little Kinnakeet, 1899). *During the same San Ciriaco hurricane of 1899, the men at Little Kinnakeet Life-Saving Station (built 1874), just a few miles south of Gull Shoal, were able to rescue seven crew members from the* Robert W. Dasey*—also driven ashore during the furious storm (see Mobley,* Ship Ashore, *124–25). The photographer Corydon Cronk took this posed picture of the station's surfmen barely a month after the heroic event. Photograph, Corydon Pirnie Cronk, 1899 (AV.5138, Carol Cronk Cole Collection, Outer Banks History Center, Manteo; this image was the original for a separate print at the State Archives of North Carolina, Raleigh [N.77.4.22, Brimley Photograph Collection]).*

4

MECCAS OF COMMERCE, FROLIC, AND SPORT

When the Wright brothers ventured to the Carolina coast for the first time in 1900, they were not sure where they would be able to procure some of their essential needs. Joseph J. Dosher had told them in his pre-arrival letter that they would not be able to rent a house in the area. He advised them to bring their own tents. William J. Tate, their first friend at Kitty Hawk—who also turned out to be their primary guide around the banks region—told them "you could fi[n]d good place to pitch Tent & get board in private family, provided there were not to[o] many in your party." So the brothers arrived at Kitty Hawk their first year—ready to camp out but with little else in hand.[1]

Unable to find a source for long pieces of spruce for the ribs of their first flying machine in Ohio, Wilbur went to the J. E. Etheridge Company mill in Norfolk on his way to Kitty Hawk, looking for the clear sturdy wood. But he ended up having to settle for white pine instead. With the help of Cumpston Goffigon at the Etheridge firm, Wilbur got the strips of pine shipped to Elizabeth City, where he also intercepted the delivery. He then transferred the wood to Israel Perry's fishing boat along with his heavy trunk. When Perry anchored in the shallow Kitty Hawk Bay on 28 September 1900, Wilbur somehow got his cargo transported to the nearby shore on shallow boats and, with the help of local residents, into the yard of Bill and Addie Tate. It was there that he would build the brothers' first flying machine.[2]

When the brothers finally moved into their tent several hundred yards from the Tate house on 4 October, they suddenly realized how complicated it was to get groceries and supplies to their encampment. Orville described their dilemma ten days later while he and Wilbur were eating a can of condensed milk for their supper: "There is no store in Kitty Hawk; that is, not anything that you would call a store." They brought along a small gasoline stove for cooking and a "bicycle gas lamp" for illumination. But they had nothing to eat unless they caught a fish or captured a squirrel. They had "no hot drink or bread or crackers" and "Will is 'most starved," he concluded.[3]

In their first year on the Carolina coast, the Wrights learned that Kitty Hawk was at one end of a complicated supply line. "Kitty Hawk is a fishing village," Orville wrote. "The people make what little living they have in fishing," he continued, shipping "tons & tons of fish away every year to Baltimore and other northern cities." Kitty Hawkers inserted fish and fowl and game and some farm products into a gigantic commercial transport system that took food and raw goods to northern cities and manufacturing centers where they were processed, consumed, or converted into finished products. The transport channels from Kitty Hawk and other coastal fishing villages and farming centers led to Elizabeth City, the hub of the Albemarle Sound region. The towns of Washington and New Bern served a similar function in Pamlico Sound. And from these towns product was sent via a network of steamboats and railroads through Norfolk onto other spokes of rail, ferry, or steamship up the Eastern Seaboard—or in some cases, back to the Midwest region whence the Wrights had come.

With a population of six thousand in 1900, Elizabeth City had emerged from the creation and confluence of a new national transportation system. It was at the southern end of the original Dismal Swamp Canal. It also had good access to the successor Albemarle and Chesapeake Canal that opened in 1859. It had critical placement near the end of the railroad lines that opened in 1881. And, in contrast with the mainly shallow waters of the Albemarle Sound, it had a deep-water port that could accommodate a number of steamships all at once ready to convey either people or cargo. Millions of fish of many varieties and tons of oysters were harvested from the sound regions and shipped out of Elizabeth City every year: "The fish are packed in ice and shipped to market fresh, except when they are taken in unusual quantities; then many of them are salted and barreled for future sales," wrote an observer, Frank Vaughan. "Millions of wild ducks, geese and swan . . . are killed in great numbers and shipped to market" as well, he continued, "this being the chief means of support of many of the [region's] inhabitants."

In addition, the Albemarle Sound area abounded with millions of acres of forests filled with pine, cypress, juniper, poplar, gum, oak, ash, maple, walnut, and hickory. Venture capitalists, "chiefly from the Middle and Northern States, have come into the district and purchased immense tracts of these forest lands," noted Vaughan. They built sawmills, spur railroads, shipping docks, steamships, kiln-drying plants—all the facilities needed to supply the world with quality woods for furniture and for trimming the corporate offices and the gray stone mansions of urban America. Steamships and spur rails pushed mountains of timber and processed lumber from Washington, Belhaven, New Bern, Manteo, Edenton, Plymouth, and other ports around the sounds (including Kitty Hawk) through Elizabeth City to hungry markets in a steady stream every day of the year.[4]

All these towns—spokes on a wheel that fed a hungry industrializing nation—were also at the ends of the line for the return of finished products—clothing, furniture, tools, building materials, and canned foods. While the brothers could not find what they needed in Kitty Hawk in 1900, when they returned in 1901 and subsequent years, they knew to bring with them from Ohio expensive items like stoves, machine parts, and custom-made rolls of cloth. They shipped these by railroad express. At Elizabeth City they got carpentry tools, building materials, grease and oil, gasoline, and nonperishable food supplies. And on the banks they bought or got game, fish, chickens and eggs, and fresh vegetables. Along with acquiring these items, they also heard an endless stream of local wisdom on how to make a living along the ribbon of sand to which they had come. The Wright brothers quickly went from thinking that they were on the edges of the earth to making full use of the remarkably advanced American business and commercial systems that had incorporated even the seemingly remote Carolina coast by 1900.

There was another dimension of the banks region that the Wrights discovered as well but that, for reasons of inclination and habit, remained only partially explored by them during their six long ventures in North Carolina. The Carolina coast had long provided playgrounds for Americans who wanted to be near the water's edge. The watery expanses also lured rich visitors who wanted to practice catching fish and hunting birds mainly for sport, not food.

By 1900 the coastal region had already been for many decades a destination for frolic and sport for many others since the plantation days of the Old South. Indeed, as early as 1850 an aspiring Philadelphia novelist by the name of George Higby Throop wrote a vivid description of the summer frolics of planters and their slaves at Nags Head beach. After spending a year or so as a schoolmaster on a plantation in nearby Bertie County, Throop penned a novel titled *Nag's Head; or Two Months among*

"The Bankers": A Story of Sea-Shore Life and Manners. Writing under the pseudonym of Gregory Seaworthy, Throop captured in diction and vivid word images the annual ritual of moving family, furniture, slaves, and social habits from Scotch Hall, the plantation mansion of Cullen Capehart on the northern edge of the Albemarle Sound, to the family's summer cottage at Nags Head. The rambling Capehart beach cottage was one of many at Nags Head that housed planter families from Hertford, Edenton, and other Albemarle Sound towns. Each day's social agenda brought the white families together for ocean bathing, fancy feasts, and dancing to musical accompaniment at a fashionable hotel—all on the sound side of the banks near Nags Head Woods. Their slaves, meanwhile, also got to know each other and to share their own stories about toils and triumphs despite the fetters of servitude. While the masters lounged with mint juleps on spacious porches, their slaves bonded while shelling clams and stewing fish chowders.[5]

After the Civil War, as these families began striving to recover their fortunes through both planting and new business enterprises, the summer frolics at Nags Head resumed—though without their slaves. The principal difference was that, beginning in 1884, many of the owners moved their cottages from the safe haven of the sound to the oceanfront—not very far from rising tides and breaking waves. Recognizing that the ocean had a caprice unknown on the sound, the relocated cottages and new ones built to accompany them were lifted onto wooden pilings above the sandy shore. With few of the architectural embellishments of their plantation homes and with a shared simplicity of structure and materials, there would be a minimal loss of investment if one of the annual storms should throw an overwash higher than the pilings. These were austere seasonal structures thrown up cheaply but with rambling space for socializing, entertaining, and porch-sitting—things these people liked to do—just as their white forefathers had long before the war. From these same porches they could watch the weekly parades of bathers who poured off the steamships that brought weekend and short-term vacationers from Norfolk, Richmond, or Washington for a brief romp at Nags Head.[6]

The Carolina coast and its inland sea had become a playground for both visitors and residents by 1903. On weekends, local fishermen converted their fishing boats into family excursion boats. Whether in their Sunday finery or picnicking garb, the year-round inhabitants of the barrier islands, towns on the sounds, or in the county seat of Manteo or the fringes of Roanoke Island went on outings. They picnicked at Fort Raleigh, took family photographs wherever they played, and enjoyed the sun and breezes that crisscrossed the islands. When Manteo's Tranquil House became a flourishing hostelry for out-of-town journalists in search of the Wright brothers and their experiments in flight, they could even get some takeout food to enjoy while looking for their prey.

While the Wright brothers never cavorted with the beachcombers at Nags Head, even they occasionally did their own beach exploring. In 1902, after finishing their flying tests for the season, Orville told Katharine, "We had lots of time to go over to the woods botanizing and looking after birds." In fact, he continued, "We went to the beach a number of times and have collected a whole bucketful of starfish besides a lot of shells and a couple of king crabs which we will bring home."[7] But there are few references among the brothers' diaries and letters to practicing the art of beachcombing.

In another realm of sport, however, that of hunting, the Wrights were avid and well-prepared participants. In fact, when they arrived at Kitty Hawk in 1900, they were barely distinguishable from the thousands of duck hunters who had been descending annually from northern climes to shoot birds on the sound side of the banks. Like the hunters who left countinghouse floors for a few weeks in Currituck country, the brothers came wearing what the locals perceived to be funny city-slicker suits and ties. Moreover, despite the local heat and humidity and working as grease monkeys on their powered machines, the brothers insisted on doing their arduous flying experiments in starched shirts and pleated pants.

Yet the Wrights never went to Kitty Hawk without taking along their own prized hunting rifle. And they used their .22 caliber repeating rifle regularly on the banks for hunting, for defense against creatures invading their camps, and for target-shooting competitions. According to Orville, writing in 1900, "This is a great country for fishing and hunting. The fish are so thick you see dozens of them whenever you look down into the water. The woods are filled with wild game. . . . At any time we look out of the tent we can see an eagle flapping its way over head, buzzards by the dozen . . . soaring over the hills and bay . . . and seagulls skimming the waves."[8] During the total of eleven months they spent on the Carolina coast between 1900 and 1911, they routinely downed birds of prey, tested their marksmanship with squirrels and mice, and took time out from flight tests to shoot at their own homemade targets.

In fact, the Wrights' self-constructed buildings that served as a combination dormitory, kitchen, and workshops much resembled the dozens of lodges up and down the banks built for teams of rich hunters. But whereas those hunters could be found in the early mornings crouched in duck blinds scattered across the shallow sounds, the Wrights were busy repairing and refining their machines for new test flights. Nevertheless, believing that a rifle was a tool, a weapon, and an instrument for competitive sport, the Wrights, like the hunters who went to the Carolina coast for a month or two each year, viewed the area as a hunter's paradise.

One expert on the sport of wild-fowl shooting, after watching the wealthy hunters in the area in 1892, wrote: "There is no place in the Union that has so many costly club-houses grouped together as Currituck Sound. Everything that could be done for the comfort and luxury of the sportsman in erecting the club-houses in this bleak, dreary region has been accomplished." The author, Alexander Hunter, during that year visited each of the two dozen or so hunt clubs that flourished from the Currituck Sound near the Virginia border all the way down to Cape Hatteras and onto Roanoke Island as well.[9]

While the wealthy clubhouse hunters pursued their sport, being treated as royalty by resident locals, the Wright brothers, in addition to shooting birds as prey, also used their gun for diverting themselves with challenges of marksmanship. In the midst of one of their most intensive, jam-packed trips to Kitty Hawk and Kill Devil Hills in 1908, the brothers still found time on a day unfit for flying to organize a shooting competition among themselves and their mechanic Charles Furnas. In typical Wright fashion, they pulled out a compass and drew up their own targets on scrap pieces of cardboard and paper. Shooting from fifty yards in a stationery position in each competition, the winner of the challenge was that brother or Furnas who in any single shot came closest to the center of the bull's eye sketched onto the target.

Finally, on the last of their expeditions to the Carolina coast in 1911, the brothers further broke from their typical austerity. While Wilbur was detained in a New York courtroom conducting one of their patent disputes, Orville and his brother Lorin along with Lorin's son Horace (nicknamed "Buster") actually hired a boat and went fishing just for amusement. Donning sombrero-styled woven hats, the Wrights headed into the fish-rich Albemarle Sound from Kill Devil Hills, cavorting like all the other people who had gone to the environs of Nags Head for centuries to enjoy the sport of fishing. Although this time of playful diversion was short-lived, even the Wrights finally enjoyed the North Carolina banks, even if for a brief moment, as a place of frolic and sport.

Kitty Hawk was a typical Carolina coastal village (Kitty Hawk, 1900). *From their first camp on the Carolina coast in 1900, the Wright brothers could see the tiny town of Kitty Hawk in the distance—as shown in this detail from a large glass plate. Kitty Hawk had the features typical of almost any coastal town—a U.S. Post Office, a dock house in the bay (distant left with the mast of a boat barely visible), a fish house for processing daily catches (on pilings in the bay above trees to right), and a single general store (structure with light gable end in center). While these provided the basic day-to-day needs of residents, they were insufficient to supply the requirements of the Wright brothers for camp goods, tools, and fuel. Glass plate negative, Wright brothers, 1900 (L568, detail, Wright Brothers Collection, Library of Congress).*

Elizabeth City—the commercial hub of the upper Carolina coast (Elizabeth City, ca. 1903). *Elizabeth City, as a railroad center and principal beneficiary of traffic passing through the Dismal Swamp Canal, and with a busy port at the headwaters of the Pasquotank River, was the transportation and business hub of the Albemarle Sound and upper banks region. By contrast with Kitty Hawk, it had the look and feel of a microcity on the make with rival mercantile enterprises and busy streets. Postcard, photographer unknown, ca. 1903 (PAS 77, Photo Collections, Museum of the Albemarle, Elizabeth City).*

Elizabeth City had quiet residential streets worth exploring (Elizabeth City, ca. 1903). *The busy entrepreneurs, merchants, and tradesmen who gathered at Elizabeth City around 1903 built impressive homes on the residential streets that radiated out from the town's transportation hub. On their many passages through the bustling town, the Wright brothers had ample time to explore the place, which more closely resembled their hometown of Dayton, Ohio, than any locale on upper coastal Carolina. Postcard, photographer unknown, ca. 1903 (PAS 43, Photo Collections, Museum of the Albemarle, Elizabeth City).*

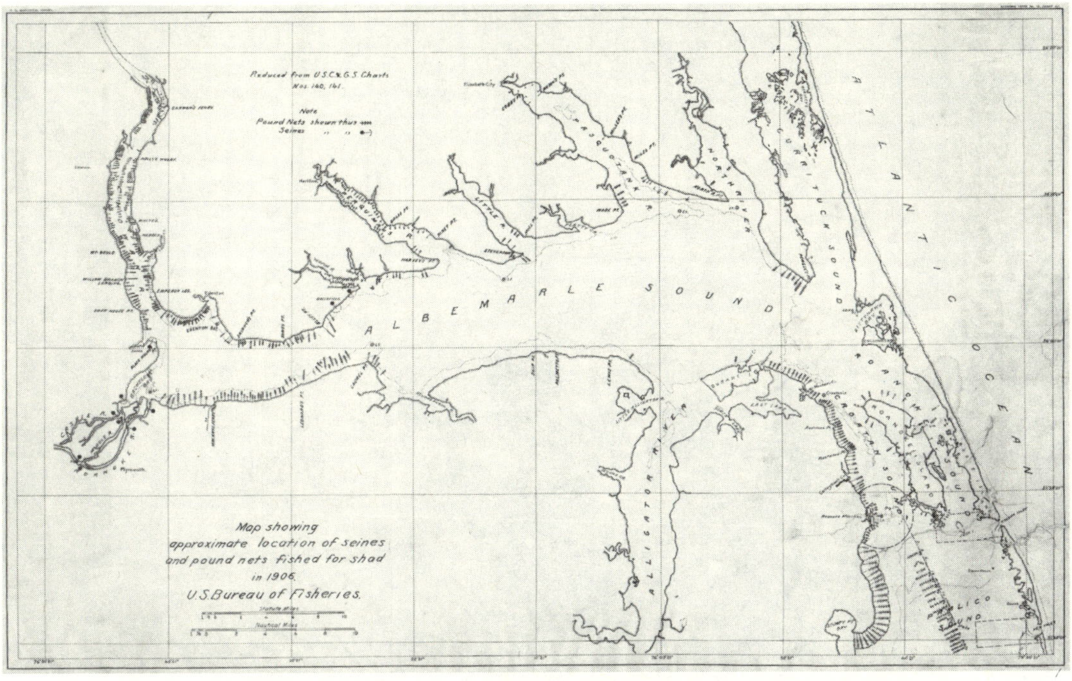

Fishing seines and pound nets around the inland sea, 1906. *The largest form of commerce on the Carolina coast was fishing. As shown in this map of the location of seines and pound nets used in harvesting shad, there were installations in abundance at the mouths of rivers and, especially, on the inland side of Croatan Sound and the perimeter of Roanoke Island. The methods of catching fish had not altered substantially from those used by the Algonquin Indians observed by English explorers in the 1580s. U.S. Bureau of Fisheries, "Location of Seines and Pound Nets Fished for Shad," 1906 (Cm912.02 1906ue, North Carolina Maps, 4868, North Carolina Collection, University of North Carolina at Chapel Hill). (For an image of how the artist John White depicted Algonquin fish weirs in 1585, see Kim Sloan,* A New World: England's First View of America *[Chapel Hill: University of North Carolina Press, 2007], 108–9.)*

Seining for mullet on the sounds (Albemarle Sound, ca. 1903). *This photograph recorded one of the small fishing operations on the Carolina sounds where men (and boys) worked close to shore to seine for mullet. In this instance, the fishing was evidently done by hand and without the use of mechanical power. The background structures in this image are unidentified. Cyanotype, photographer unknown, ca. 1903 (10000238, Photo Collections, North Carolina Museum of Natural Sciences, Raleigh).*

Purse seining for menhaden in the sounds (Albemarle Sound, 1884). *Another form of seining was to deploy a long net between two shallow boats and ensnare large numbers of fish as the craft headed to shore pulling the ends of the net. The men in this picture were described by observers from the North Carolina Museum of Natural Sciences as seining for a writhing school of menhaden. Glass plate negative, photographer unknown, 1884 (10000153.N027, Photo Collections, North Carolina Museum of Natural Sciences, Raleigh).*

Every person could devise a homemade fishing trap (Albemarle Sound, ca. 1903). *North Carolina naturalists traveling around the Carolina sounds at the turn of the twentieth century observed and photographed a multiplicity of fish-catching devices, many of them resembling the stationary fishing weirs employed by native Indians—and much envied by English explorers in the sixteenth century. Photograph, photographer unknown, ca. 1903 (PhC42 Bx12F13, Brimley Photograph Collection, State Archives of North Carolina, Raleigh).*

Large-scale commercial fishing operations were there, too (Albemarle Sound, ca. 1903). *Naturalists and travelers could also visit a variety of large-scale fishing operations with teams of sturdy men from a wide diversity of backgrounds whose job it was to draw in huge nets to the docks of fish-processing plants where freshly caught fish were sorted, iced, and packaged for immediate transshipment to the outer world. Photograph, photographer unknown, ca. 1903 (PhC42 Bx12F41, Brimley Photograph Collection, State Archives of North Carolina, Raleigh).*

Crates of iced fish ready for transfer to boats or trains (Albemarle Sound, ca. 1903). *Crated or boxed fish from processing plants at Belhaven, Manteo, Plymouth, Edenton—or even Kitty Hawk—got transferred most often to the shipping center at Elizabeth City to be transported by rail or steamboat to awaiting markets in northern cities. Photograph, photographer unknown, 1903 (PhC42 Bx12F9, Brimley Photograph Collection, State Archives of North Carolina, Raleigh).*

Small-scale logging around the Carolina sounds (Roanoke Island, ca. 1903). *North Carolina's abundant forests around the Albemarle and Pamlico Sounds were harvested commercially by outside timber investors. Smaller stands of timber on farmlands were extracted log by log, as here on Roanoke Island, by local people and hauled to sawmills to be sliced into rough-cut boards for use in constructing barns and outbuildings on family farms. Photograph, photographer unknown, ca. 1903 (PC.5126-13-152-153, D. Victor Meekins Collection, Outer Banks History Center, Manteo).*

Saw mill operations proliferated for rip-cutting timber (Dare County, ca. 1903). *Beginning in the 1890s sawmills for both home consumption and out-shipment sprang up to rip logs into rough lumber to be stacked for either air or kiln drying. The waste from such cutting (bark slabs) are piled beside this sawmill to be used for firewood or other temporary outbuildings such as pigpens and chicken houses. Photograph, photographer unknown, ca. 1903 (PhC42 Bx13F4, Brimley Photograph Collection, State Archives of North Carolina, Raleigh).*

Commercial timber operators leveled many forest lands (Pasquotank County, ca. 1903). *Large-scale timber operators installed industrial-scale facilities for transferring logs between rivercrafts and railroad cars. This fixed crane swiveled large timbers onto awaiting railroad cars to be carried away to other markets for construction projects or to be shaved and molded into fine grains for making furniture. Photograph, photographer unknown, ca. 1903 (F 1-1911, State Agency Records, Forestry Resources Group, Forestry Collection, Pasquotank County, State Archives of North Carolina, Raleigh).*

Elizabeth City had plenty of grocers and dry-goods merchants (Elizabeth City, ca. 1903). *People around Albemarle Sound used Elizabeth City as the region's center for the purchase of dry goods and processed food supplies. The Wright brothers always stocked up in places like this store on onions, potatoes, and many canned goods (especially vegetables and condensed milk) on their way to Kitty Hawk. Photograph, photographer unknown, ca. 1903 (1992-141-6, Photo Collections, Museum of the Albemarle, Elizabeth City).*

Lumber, roofing, and nails also came from Elizabeth City (Elizabeth City, ca. 1903). *Elizabeth City's venerable Kramer Brothers Lumber Company hewed, cured, and sawed piles of lumber for every building. The Kramer Company took the Wright brothers' lists of building material needs and shipped the products to them via Kitty Hawk (usually on Capt. Franklin Harris Midgett's boats) to their camp at Kill Devil Hills. Photograph, photographer unknown, ca. 1903 (PAS 310, Photo Collections, Museum of the Albemarle, Elizabeth City).*

The Wright brothers' orderly and well-stocked kitchen (Kill Devil Hill, 1902). *This image of the Wright brothers' kitchen was made in 1902, the day after they completed the construction of a new camp building and installed a new gas stove and a small oilcloth-covered table that they built on the site. The groceries, dry goods, sacks of sugar and flour, and canned vegetables they had just bought in Elizabeth City—as well as the cheap china, lanterns, and cooking implements they got at a general store there—had just been neatly shelved. Photograph, Wright brothers, 1902 (15-7-22, Wright Brothers Collection, Paul C. Dunbar Library, Wright State University, Dayton, Ohio). (For further analysis and detailed photos of the many items contained in this photograph, see Larry E. Tise,* Hidden Images: Discovering Details in the Wright Brothers' Kitty Hawk Photographs, 1900–1911 *[Charleston: History Press, 2005], 64–65.)*

Converting boards into barrier island buildings (Kill Devil Hill, 1908). *As was the custom locally, the Wright brothers proudly built most of their crude camp buildings with their own hands. For their 1908 camp, shown in this image, the brothers salvaged lumber from their damaged 1903 camp buildings (left). But they also brought in a shipment of freshly cut lumber from Elizabeth City to build a sturdy new building (right). Glass plate negative, Wright brothers, 1908 (L673, Wright Brothers Collection, Library of Congress).*

Weekend vacationers took steamboat excursions to Nags Head, ca. 1903. *The most popular place for weekend or weeklong excursions on the banks was the well-established resort of Nags Head. Since the 1840s, when steamboats began making regular calls at Nags Head, people from Norfolk and beyond could make short trips to the beach setting and lodge at a fancy hotel. By the turn of the twentieth century, travelers had their choice of multiple rail and steamboat connections traveling via Elizabeth City, usually with a brief stop in Manteo. Photograph, photographer unknown, ca. 1903 (PC.5001.5-47.011, David Stick Collection, Outer Banks History Center, Manteo).*

Manteo became the commercial crossroads for the Carolina sounds (Manteo, 1908). *Manteo, the principal town on Roanoke Island and the county seat for Dare County (which included most of the northern barrier banks), had become the commercial and transportation crossroads of the Carolina sounds by ca. 1903. The busy docks on Shallowbag Bay are shown in this panoramic view taken by the renowned photographer James Hare in 1908. Lantern slide, James Hare, 1908 (1520.640, James Hare Collection, Harry Ransom Research Center, University of Texas at Austin).*

Manteo was accessible only by water (Manteo, 1908). *Manteo was the county seat for Dare County, containing most of the barrier island chain of the upper banks region. The county's newly completed 1904 courthouse is the building with the cupola pictured on the right. The Kitty Hawk U.S. Weather Station was also closed and moved to Manteo that same year. The new weather station's communications tower is visible just to the left of the courthouse tower. Lantern slide, James Hare, 1908 (1500.622, James Hare Collection, Harry Ransom Research Center, University of Texas at Austin).*

Fishing boats also made good family-outing craft (sound region, ca. 1903). *Given the abundance of boats and boating know-how around the Carolina sounds and along the coast, there were many compelling reasons to take the same vessels out on a Sunday afternoon excursion, given a beautiful day and calm waters. Photograph, photographer unknown, ca. 1903 (PhC42 Bx6F18, Brimley Photograph Collection, State Archives of North Carolina, Raleigh).*

An excursion to the Fort Raleigh landing was a popular trip (Roanoke Island, ca. 1903). *Some family outings included landings along the much-eroded northern end of Roanoke Island near the spot where Raleigh's colonists had built fortifications and family dwellings in the 1580s. Photograph, photographer unknown, ca. 1903 (PC.5126-13.135, D. Victor Meekins Collection, Outer Banks History Center, Manteo).*

Childhood memories got recorded at Fort Raleigh monument (Fort Raleigh, ca. 1903). *The Fort Raleigh monument instantly became a recreation spot where a boy's or girl's most memorable childhood photograph might be snapped, inscribed, and preserved for a lifetime of recollections. Photograph, photographer unknown, ca. 1903 (PC.5126-13-23, D. Victor Meekins Collection, Outer Banks History Center, Manteo. Note that this prized family print was made from a reversed negative before the addition of a notation memorializing a family outing.)*

Picture taking was a diversion in and of itself (Cape Hatteras, 1899). *Since portable cameras outside of photographic studios were a relatively new phenomenon on the Carolina coast ca. 1903, taking family or community photographs was an entertaining event enjoyed by many. In this photograph taken from the balcony of the Cape Hatteras Weather Station in 1899, it appears that a family has donned dress-up clothes—perhaps on a Sunday afternoon—for a somewhat distant group portrait. Photograph, Corydon Pirnie Cronk, 1899 (AV.5138, Carol Cronk Cole Collection, Outer Banks History Center, Manteo).*

A group photographic portrait at the Tranquil House (Manteo, ca. 1903). *Another popular place for a family picture-taking session—including all the matriarchs and patriarchs of a family—was the front porch of the Tranquil House hotel in downtown Manteo. In this dramatically posed portrait, two of the men appear to be holding hunting rifles. Photograph, photographer unknown, ca. 1903 (AV.5205.3.074, Manteo Centennial Exhibition Photograph Collection, Outer Banks History Center, Manteo).*

Takeout food was available from the Tranquil House (advertisement, ca. 1903). *In addition to serving as a setting for family photographs and a hostel for visitors passing through Manteo, the Tranquil House provided baskets of takeout food for individuals making day trips from the hotel to Fort Raleigh, to Nags Head, or even over to Kill Devil Hills to observe the experimental flights of the Wright brothers. Newspaper advertisement, ca. 1903 (AV.5205, Manteo Centennial Exhibition Photograph Collection, Outer Banks History Center, Manteo).*

An important day trip from the Tranquil House (Kill Devil Hills, 1908). *This group of reporters from New York set out from the Tranquil House with a lunch basket one morning in May 1908 to cover a new round of secret flights being attempted by the Wright brothers at Kill Devil Hills. In this rare photograph, the reporters had arrived on the sound side of the banks and were trudging across the arid sands behind Big Kill Devil Hill. Lantern slide, James H. Hare, 1908 (1505.627, James Hare Collection, Harry Ransom Research Center, University of Texas at Austin). (For a thorough narrative of what was written about the Wright brothers' flights in 1908, see Larry E. Tise,* Conquering the Sky: The Secret Flights of the Wright Brothers at Kitty Hawk *[New York: Palgrave Macmillan, 2009].)*

Lying in wait for a Wright brothers' flight (Kill Devil Hills, 1908). *The Wrights hoped to make their experimental flights in 1908 in private—away from the prying eyes of reporters and photographers. Assignment reporters and the photographer James Hare thus had to hide all day among scruff oaks near the brothers' flying field. By the time this picture was taken, their Tranquil House lunch basket had been emptied. Photograph, James H. Hare, 1908 (17-1-16, Wright Brothers Collection, Paul C. Dunbar Library, Wright State University, Dayton, Ohio).*

Hunter and marksman Orville Wright (Kill Devil Hill, 1911). *The Wright brothers always had a rifle with them at their North Carolina camps and used it both for hunting and in marksmanship competitions during breaks in flying experiments. In this image Orville Wright is shown cleaning his rifle in the kitchen corner of the brothers' 1911 camp building. An analysis of this photograph by forensic firearm professionals suggested that this gun was probably a Marlin Repeating Rifle Model 1892, which could be purchased from the* Sears Roebuck Catalogue *in 1902 for $10.40. (See Tom Trochum and Neil Morin, forensic firearm and tool mark examiners, "Examination of Wright Brothers' Targets," 20 November 2009, typed manuscript [author's personal collection]). Photograph, probably Lorin Wright, 1911 (42-14, Wright Family Collection, Paul C. Dunbar Library, Wright State University, Dayton, Ohio).*

The hunt club at New Inlet (New Inlet, 1899). *The hunt clubs along Currituck Sound—most of them built by rich and worldly folk from both northern and southern cities—could be simple and plain on the exterior but plenty comfortable for members on the interior. This hunt club building at New Inlet (photographed by Corydon Cronk right after the San Ciriaco hurricane of 1899), with its firmly shuttered windows, obviously survived the storm's fury. Photograph, Corydon Pirnie Cronk, 1899 (AV.5138, Carol Cronk Cole Collection, Outer Banks History Center, Manteo).*

Coastal hunt clubs were managed by local guides (sounds region, ca. 1903). *North Carolina's dozens of hunt clubs of all sizes, shapes, and levels of comfort and elegance were managed and maintained by well-paid local guides. These experienced hands, with the assistance of low-paid local black servants who handled the kill and cooked, maintained the club buildings. The guides were also responsible for producing local helpers, ammunition, and dogs, and for training visiting hunters in the arts of gunning during the annual late-fall migrations of waterfowl along the U.S. coast. Photograph, perhaps H. H. Brimley, ca. 1903 (PhC42 Bx17F7, Brimley Photograph Collection, State Archives of North Carolina, Raleigh).*

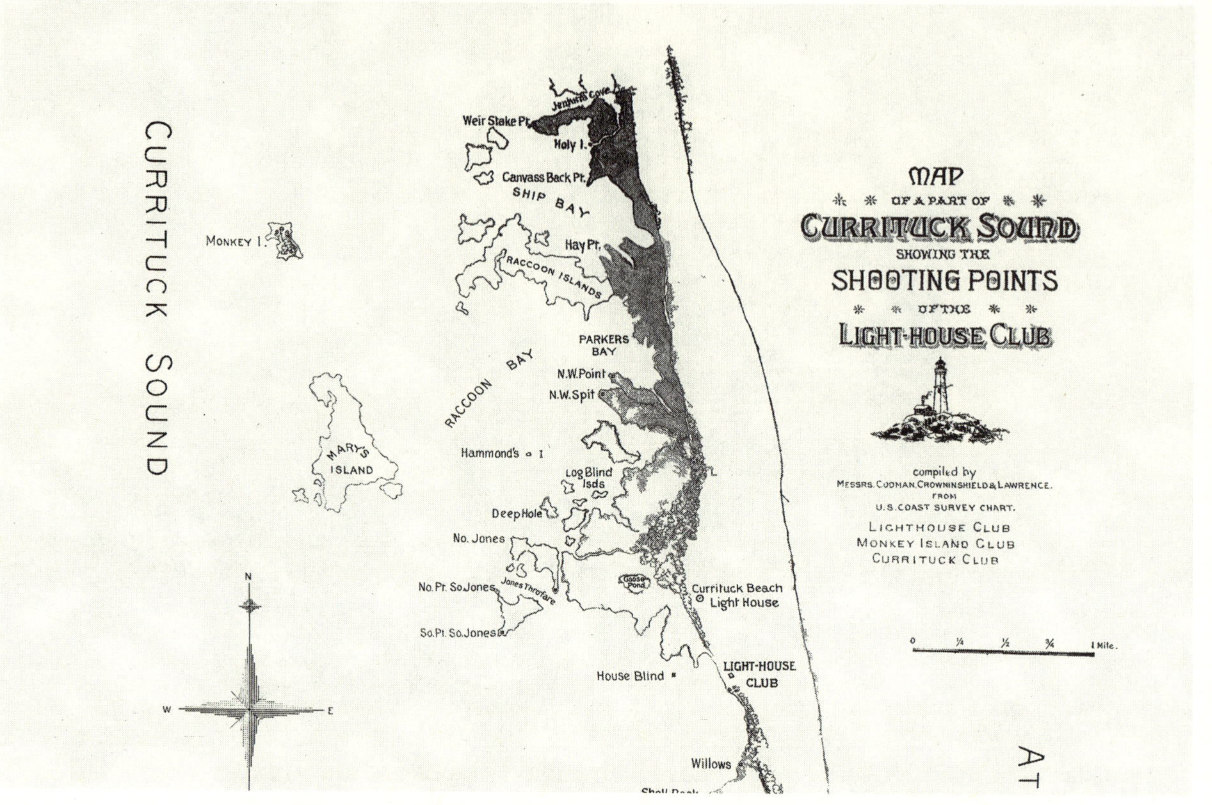

The "shooting points" of the Light-House Club at Corolla (Currituck Sound, ca. 1880s). *Three "Boston Brahmin" loved their hunting club—the Light-House Club at Corolla—so much that they sketched and printed a map of their favorite spots around Currituck Sound to bag geese. The authors of the map were "Messrs. Codman, Crowninshield, & Lawrence"—probably the famous architect Ogden Codman Jr. (1863–1951), the wealthy yacht-racer and marksman Francis Boardman Crowninshield (1869–1950), and the Episcopal bishop of Massachusetts William Lawrence (1850–1941) (See "Boston Brahmin,"* Wikipedia, *http://en.wikipedia.org/wiki/Ogden_Codman_Jr.; http://en.wikipedia.org/wiki//Louise_E._du_Pont_Crowninshield; http://en.wikipedia.org/wiki//William_Lawrence,_1850-1941 [accessed 29 January 2014]). Detail of Messrs. Codman, Crowninshield, and Lawrence, "Map of a Part of Currituck Sound Showing the Shooting Points of the Light-House Club" (reprint, n.d., Whalehead Club Preservation Trust, Currituck, North Carolina).*

Exhibiting the catch and the kill (probably Craven County, ca. 1903). *One of the oldest rituals of humankind, especially fishermen and hunters, is to exhibit the size of the catch or the volume of the kill. With the development of portable cameras, a photograph of the fisherman or hunter with his or her fish or game became the proof of prowess and success. The young boy in this photograph was likely not the hunter but rather the designated guardian of the day's prizes from man and beast. Photograph, probably H. H. Brimley, ca. 1903 (10000240, Photo Collections, North Carolina Museum of Natural Sciences, Raleigh).*

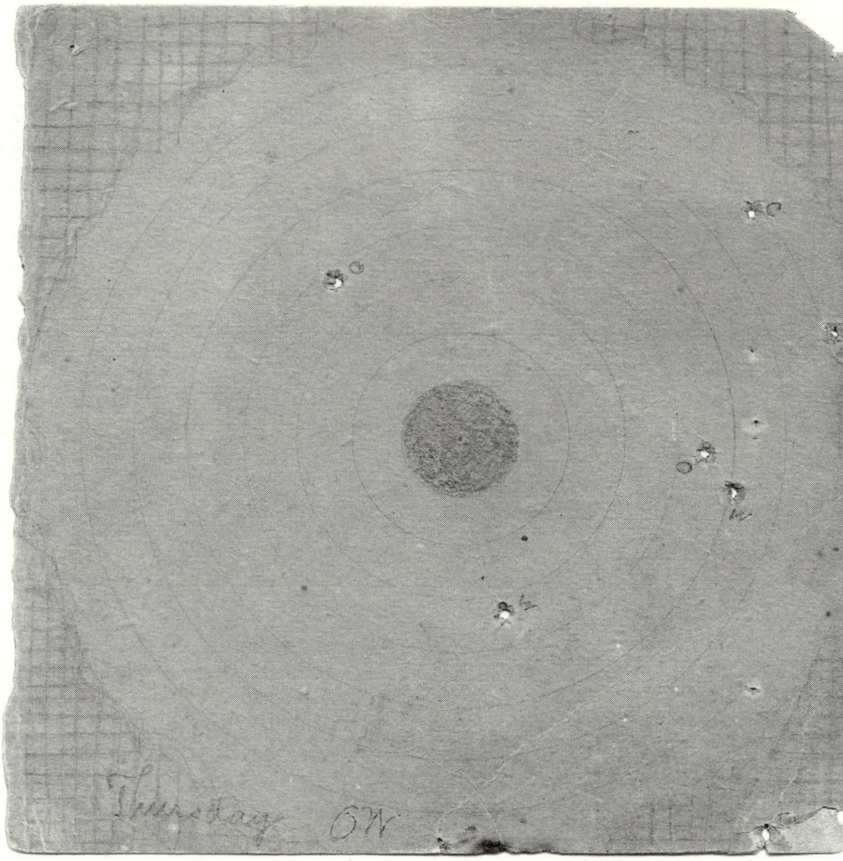

The Wrights made their targets for shooting competitions (Kill Devil Hill, 1908). *The brothers made their own targets from scraps of paper or cardboard—such as this "Thursday" target (i.e., the day it was used) from 1908. Orville ("OW") was the best marksman that day. The competition included Orville ("O"), Wilbur ("W"), and their mechanic from Dayton, Ohio, Charles Furnas ("C"). Each of them took three shots from a standing position at a distance of fifty yards. The shooter getting closest to the center of the bull's eye that day was declared the winner. Paper target, Wright brothers, 1908; photograph by Joseph Barricella, East Carolina University, 2010 (Wright Brothers Target Collection, Twiddy and Company, Corolla, North Carolina).*

Even the Wright brothers went fishing occasionally (Albemarle Sound, 1911). *While the stern taskmaster brother, Wilbur, was stuck in a New York court defending the Wrights' flying machine patent in 1911, two other Wright brothers—Orville and Lorin—went fishing between flight tests. In this photograph taken on a rented fishing boat, Lorin (left), Orville (background), and Lorin's son Horace (foreground) return from a day of fishing in the Albemarle Sound. The brothers protected their balding heads with straw hats. Photograph, probably Alec Ogilvie, 1911 (42-16, Wright Family Collection, Paul C. Dunbar Library, Wright State University, Dayton, Ohio).*

5

OF PEOPLE AND PREJUDICE

At 1:30 a.m. on the morning of 25 September 1903—on their way to Kill Devil Hills to make the first powered flight in human history—Wilbur and Orville Wright checked into the Tranquil House hotel in Manteo, North Carolina. This was their first trip from Elizabeth City to their testing grounds by way of Manteo, the county seat of Dare County. Located on Roanoke Island and accessible only by water, Manteo was also a crossroads for boat and ferry traffic across and between North Carolina's coastal sounds. At the geographic and historic heart of the upper reaches of the Carolina coast, residents and visitors alike could look east across the waters of Roanoke Sound and see cottages at Nags Head as well as the towering sandy dunes adjacent to Nags Head Woods and even the more distant dunes at Kill Devil Hills.

Manteo, recently made the courthouse town for Dare County, was additionally becoming the symbolic center and pilgrimage site to pay homage to the beginnings of English America. The Commonwealth of Virginia was gearing up in 1907 for a festive three hundredth anniversary of the first permanent English settlement in what was to become the United States at Jamestown. Meanwhile, ardent promoters of tourism and business on the Carolina coast were hoping to trump the Jamestown story with the saga of Sir Walter Raleigh's lost colony. Just a few miles west of Manteo on the northern coast of Roanoke Island was the presumed site of Fort Raleigh, where Raleigh's colonies had made the very first English imprint on American soil in the 1580s. It was not without a measure of historical poetry that at the very moment the Wright brothers were opening the doors to a new world of flight a few miles east of Manteo, others nearby were seeking to celebrate the earliest days of European exploration and settlement of what they called "the new found land of Virginia."

Much overlooked and already nearly suppressed or forgotten by 1903 was the setting nearby of yet another landmark event in American history. In early February 1862, Union and Confederate troops and their gunboats clashed for control of the strategically located Roanoke Island. The much larger Union forces, who carried out here one of the first amphibious assaults in history, overwhelmed and routed the small but feisty Confederate contingent of men and gunboats guarding the entrance to the Albemarle Sound. The victorious General Ambrose Burnside, commander of the Union army in that sector, established his headquarters barely a stone's throw from where Raleigh's colonists had eked out their existence. Through a turn of historic irony the Union encampment became an instant magnet attracting thousands of slaves fleeing eastern North Carolina plantations in search of liberty. To accommodate the horde of refugees designated by Union commanders as contraband, Union officials threw up some hastily constructed buildings and called the new village a "Freedman's Colony." Thus juxtaposed were the places where English imperialists sought to colonize the New World and where American slaves three centuries later sought shelter from their slaveholding English descendants.

If ever the Wright brothers were going to engage with these significant dramas of American history that played out on the Carolina coast, it would have been on their trips to Manteo in 1903, 1908, and 1911, during their several stays at the town's Tranquil House. The widely praised Tranquil House was a handsome and comfortable hostel for well-heeled travelers. It was also the favorite lodgment for the dozen or so reporters and photographers who went in chase of the Wright brothers in 1908 and 1911 seeking to get a juicy story or perchance a photograph of the latest flying machine devised, by then, by the world's most famous aeronauts. The popular hotel was also the place where pilgrims slept as they made worshipful visits at the turn of the century to the birthplace of English America and to the celebrated birthplace of Virginia Dare, the first English child born and baptized in North America.

Sojourners at the Tranquil House—including the Wrights—could not fail to be reminded of this story being vaunted at the time as a centerpiece of this White Anglo-Saxon Protestant epic for the rise of the American nation. What were described as the original ballast stones for one of Raleigh's ships from the 1580s were piled in the front yard of the hotel. Nor could Tranquil House guests pass down Manteo's unpaved streets without noting the presence of the town's numerous busy and hardworking black residents. Black farmers could be observed hauling boxes of produce on wagons or carts pulled by horses or oxen to the Manteo docks on Shallowbag Bay. Black boatmen and fishermen were on the docks ready to assist in loading the commercial vessels that made calls at Manteo, to take visitors out fishing, or to taxi transients who needed a ride over to Nags Head, Colington Island, or even Kill Devil Hills. And if the Wright brothers had followed the track of many other visitors in those years out of Manteo over to Fort Raleigh, they would have seen black farmers tilling their fields, black women and children harvesting berries and turnips, and strapping black boys and men hauling logs to sawmills.[1]

But what could not be so easily seen or discerned during a stroll about the town of Manteo was a dangerous undercurrent of hatred and strife that was going on at the time between the black and white citizens of coastal Carolina. The entire expanse of northeastern North Carolina was abuzz in 1900 with a massive, mean, and often harsh rearrangement in the conduct of human affairs. It had been just thirty-five years since the end of the Civil War—but a brief moment in the arc of human history. Yet those war years had been a time of revolutionary social upheaval on the Carolina coast. While the Battle of Roanoke Island, which brought Union control to the northern coast of North Carolina and freed thousands of slaves, is little noted in most accounts of the Civil War, it unleashed an internal struggle among white North Carolinians regarding which president they would obey—Abraham Lincoln or Jefferson Davis. It also inaugurated a complete transformation in the relationship between white and black residents up and down the state's watery coast.

As eastern North Carolina's slave-based society shattered, the overnight emergence of the large Freedman's Colony on Roanoke Island starkly posed the question of where emancipated blacks would live after the war and how they would relate to their former masters. As the colony of ex-slaves mushroomed to 3,500 residents, Union army recruiters enlisted hundreds of young black men into "colored" regiments that were soon deployed to fields of battle across the Confederate South. When the war came to an end, there were still dozens of wooden dormitories built in neat rows to house the black families who came there for refuge and freedom. But within two years after the war ended—despite animated black protests—the Freedman's Colony residents were dispersed back to the towns and counties from which they had fled during the war. The hope of Reconstruction governors was that these newly emancipated Americans would be able to pursue new lives in their former homes as freedmen in a cleansed southern society.[2]

But while former slaves hoped to become full-fledged citizens after the war, many states, north and south, enacted Jim Crow laws segregating whites and blacks in most public arenas. From the years of Reconstruction until the end of the nineteenth century—whether through new legal barriers or intimidation—black Americans were forced into a much-restricted realm of second-class citizenship. Their fate during this chapter of a brutal drama seemed to be condoned by the U.S. Supreme Court in its 1896 landmark decision *Plessy v. Ferguson*, which approved separate but equal schools and public facilities for whites and blacks across America.

This blow against the equal participation of blacks in American society was followed, at least in North Carolina, in 1898 by a white-supremacy campaign waged by Democrats that swept their Republican opponents out of elective office and eliminated black voters from the body politic. The ultimate meaning of this repressive second political and social revolution was clearly demonstrated at the southern end of the North Carolina coast in the city of Wilmington in 1898, where white supremacists used bloody force to expel people of color not only from government and voting but also from any formal role in the city's society. What was at the time described by white editors as the "Wilmington race riots" of 1898 was for all practical purposes the overthrow of a duly elected black-led government by an armed band of white subversives.[3]

Thus, when the Wright brothers arrived on the coast of North Carolina in 1900, the full and sometimes bloody deed of forced segregation had just been accomplished—at least politically—and was in the process of being worked out through a statewide system of segregated public schools, separate waiting rooms for whites and "colored" people in train stations, and separate train cars for whites and blacks. Black Carolinians had already established their own churches with their own black clergy in affiliation with such black-operated religious denominations as the African Methodist Episcopal or African Methodist Episcopal Zion Churches or their correlates in the Baptist and Presbyterian faiths. Despite the creation of separate churches, schools, and public accommodations, white and black men still worked side by side in the fishing and lumbering businesses scattered around the Carolina sounds. It was in the realm of agriculture—small farms—that they toiled separately. It was still an era of subsistence farming, at least along the Carolina coast, where white and black families tilled their separate fields. With perhaps one modest cash crop—corn, sweet potatoes, or tobacco—most of the energies of all farmers went into feeding their families and making a few extra dollars to buy clothes, tools, and seeds for the next year's crops.

Coming as the Wright brothers did from a northern clime, one might expect that they would have commented on the draconian separation of races that was emerging in eastern North Carolina. But they did not. In all their hundreds of letters and thousands of diary entries relating to their North Carolina experiences, not once did they make reference to the process of segregation and subjugation that was occurring. This can be explained in part by the fact that the brothers were in North Carolina for a singular purpose not related to reforming, that is to fly, not to rehabilitate society. But they were also social and political conservatives reflecting the values of their right-leaning Republican father, Bishop Milton Wright. Yet even more important, their hometown of Dayton, Ohio, had already gone through the process of segregating blacks from white society.

Although the renowned black poet Paul Laurence Dunbar had once been Orville Wright's classmate at Dayton's Central High School, the Dayton schools had also been segregated in 1893. Additionally, black men and women were almost uniformly barred from working in any of Dayton's newly emerging industries. Although the Wright family did employ a black laundress (Lottie Jones), domestic work was one of only two occupations (servant or launderer) open to black women in Dayton around 1900. And when the brothers established their own airplane manufacturing company in 1909, they adhered to local Dayton racial practices. There is no evidence that they ever employed blacks in any capacity at the firm.[4]

The Wright brothers' silent conformance to a segregated society was demonstrated in other ways when they went to the Carolina coast. Despite the fact that they took pictures of many people and places and commented on most of the people they encountered, they made no pictures of blacks, and they were virtually silent on matters of race, color, and white prejudices. They seemed to have tin ears on the subject and readily participated in the use of racial stereotypes common to their era. For example, when Orville became exasperated with an invasion of wild pigs in their Kill Devil Hills camp in 1902, he commented in his diary: "I made a 'nigger shooter' and am anxiously awaiting the appearance of a pig." Evidently, in Dayton society such was the informal name for a slingshot.[5]

While the Wrights were mainly silent on the segregating direction of American society, they did at least exhibit a passing familiarity with the story of Sir Walter Raleigh's lost colony. Although there is no indication that either of the brothers made a trek over to the site of Fort Raleigh, Orville was evidently thinking about the story of Raleigh's misplaced colony when the brothers arrived at their old camp in 1903. As he surveyed their weather-damaged 1902 building, which was "several feet nearer the ocean than when we left last year, and about a foot lower, in places," he was reminded of a major storm he and Wilbur had experienced at Kill Devil Hills in 1901. According to Orville, that was "when the wind at a speed of 107 miles per hour took the anemometer cups away with it . . . and when the mosquitoes were so thick as to dim the very brightness of the sun, exceeding in number all excepting those that devoured the whole of Raleigh's settlers on Roanoke."[6]

While the brothers exhibited little interest in either the rich history of the Carolina coast or the uneasy relations between whites and blacks, newspaper accounts of their daring successes in December 1903 may have inspired at least one black North Carolinian who was deeply focused at that moment on both history and the problems of race. Edward A. Johnson (1860–1944), an energetic lawyer and Republican politician in Raleigh, was deeply offended by the white supremacy revolution of 1898 in North Carolina. Having proved his abilities as an entrepreneur, a real estate developer, and professor of law at Raleigh's Shaw University, Johnson took a cue from the flying exploits of the Wrights and others in 1903 to imagine a world that would eventually be free of racial bigotry. In a book titled *Light Ahead for the Negro*, written and published in 1904, Johnson employed a literary tool much like that used a few years later by the renowned author H. G. Wells in his own futuristic novel *War in the Air* (1908).[7]

In Wells's novel, the central figure, Bert Smallways, a young British subject, is captured and forced aboard a German airship where he is put to sleep.[8] When he wakes up, the German flying craft is in its final approach to conduct a bombing raid on New York City. Smallways comes back to consciousness in a world where warfare is conducted in the air and not on land. In Johnson's novel, the central figure is Gilbert Twitchell, a white recent graduate of Yale University who is determined to spend his life among Negroes in the South, "helping to fit them for the new citizenship that had developed as a result of the war." Twitchell departs in 1906 for Georgia, also by airship, from a new aerial pier at the foot of West Fifty-Ninth Street in New York City. His plane crashes en route leaving him unconscious somewhere in Georgia. But whereas Wells's Smallways wakes up just days later, Johnson's Twitchell wakes up a century later, in 2006. When Twitchell regains consciousness, he learns that southern whites have moved to northern cities for manufacturing jobs, leaving their abandoned lands to be acquired by black farmers. Therefore, the southerners he encounters are barely aware of the old racial hatreds. American society had long ago decided to adhere to the Golden Rule of Christianity. Despite the futuristic elements of Johnson's novel, Twitchell recounts step by step and incident by incident the process whereby white supremacists had violently subjugated blacks in North Carolina after the Civil War.[9]

While Edward Johnson was using the idea of flight to meditate on the problem of race at Raleigh's Shaw University in 1903, another Raleigh habitué, the state's lieutenant governor, Francis D. Winston (1857–1941), chose another coastal Carolina story line a few years later—that of Raleigh's first settlements on Roanoke Island—to explain his version of what was happening between the races in the same time period. Whereas Johnson had put his interpretation of events in a thinly veiled novel, Winston put his story into oratory—something for which he was well known. The occasion for his pronouncement was one of those almost cultic commemorations of the miraculous birth of Virginia Dare—the first English child born in North America—held on 20 May 1908. The setting for his performance was, quite notably, the site of Fort Raleigh near Manteo, which by the early years of the twentieth century was becoming a primary place to celebrate the accomplishments of the white race in America.

Although Lieutenant Governor Winston came from Bertie County, which borders the Albemarle Sound, and had been a leading North Carolina Republican proponent of black political participation after the Civil War, he switched to the Democratic Party in the 1890s and became one of the chief architects of the state's white supremacy campaigns of 1898 and 1900. He even organized what he called "White government unions" across the state to push black voters out of the political process.[10]

In fact, just as Winston and his fellow white supremacists went to work in North Carolina in the 1890s to establish white control of the political process, another organization, the Roanoke Colony Memorial Association, was formed to mark the place where white Anglo-Saxons had made their first incursion into North America. The association, made up chiefly of North Carolina Episcopalians and a few historians, had dedicated a stark granite marker at the traditional site of Fort Raleigh on 24 November 1896. Placed on a parcel of land newly acquired by the association, the marker bore an inscription commemorating the place where "the first settlers of the English race" had put down roots in America, where the first English child in America was born, and where the "first known celebrations of a Christian sacrament" (the baptisms of Virginia Dare and the Indian chief Manteo) occurred.

The granite monument celebrating white achievements instantly became the most visited historic site in the upper coastal region of North Carolina. From the moment it was dedicated, families up and down coastal Carolina used the tiny site as a gathering place for family outings. When portable still cameras came into vogue, the marker became a favored setting for family photographs and for still shots of children, who would remember the occasion as long as they lived. The popularity of the site increased markedly after the North Carolina author Sallie Southall Cotten (1846–1929) published her beloved epic poem *The White Doe: The Fate of Virginia Dare, an Indian Legend* (1901). By putting Virginia Dare in the form of a young female deer, Cotten gave an eternal imaginary presence on the Carolina coast for the firstborn English child.[11]

By the time Lieutenant Governor Winston made his 1908 pronouncements on the remarkable history of the white race, the site had already achieved a recognized level of both historical and symbolic significance. But he added more import to the site. First of all, the date for the commemoration was not Virginia Dare's birth date (18 August) but rather 20 May, the date of the supposed Mecklenburg Declaration of Independence, when in 1775 rebellious firebrands in Charlotte, North Carolina—all white men—gathered to declare their independence from England. It was also, not by coincidence, the date—20 May 1861—when North Carolina declared its independence from the Union and joined the Confederate States of America.

To add a further element of real coincidental luster to the 1908 commemoration, it occurred the very week the Wright brothers finished the most important secret flights they ever conducted at Kill Devil Hills. Wilbur Wright, as it happened, was at the Tranquil House the night before the commemoration at Fort Raleigh as he raced from North Carolina to France to demonstrate to a waiting world how to fly. The New York and world reporters who descended on Manteo to cover the covert experiments of the Wright brothers were still lurking about filing their stories at the Manteo telegraph office next door to the Tranquil House. And they kept on taking photographs. Orville remained encamped at the foot of Big Kill Devil Hill. In a quite odd but literal sense, past, present, and future merged in the town of Manteo at the Tranquil House in May 1908. The Wright brothers went forth from Manteo that month to fly publicly for the first time ever and to secure their place in the history of flight. Another group of innovators descended on Manteo and Roanoke Island to launch their story of how the white race had conquered North America on those very grounds and would be forever commemorated through the tragic story of Sir Walter Raleigh's lost colony and its firstborn white child.

On the auspicious morning of 20 May 1908, an assembly of high church Episcopalians from across North Carolina sailed on the steamer *Virginia* from Elizabeth City to the northern shore of Roanoke Island en route to Fort Raleigh, where they planned to commemorate both the birth of Virginia Dare and "the endeavors of the brave men who made the attempt at settlement on Roanoke." From the ferry "the company was carried ashore in Roanoke shad boats—very picturesque indeed," wrote the scribe who published the official report of the pilgrimage. Once the group arrived at the site of the granite monument, a program of religious and civil services got under way. After the prayers and sermons concluded, Bishop Robert Strange introduced North Carolina's Lieutenant Governor Francis D. Winston as "the special orator of the day."[12]

Leaving no stone unturned, Winston described in stirring detail the conquest of America by a superior English race. Sir Walter Raleigh was more than an explorer; he was a great planter. "Raleigh's colony on Roanoke Island was the first planting of the English race in America," proclaimed Winston. "It [the colony] came for that purpose; others had come before, but not to plant a race." The planting of the race was fulfilled in the birth of Virginia Dare. When she was born on Roanoke Island, there "was heard the cry of an infant child, of pure Caucasian blood, proclaiming the birth of the white race on the western hemisphere."[13]

Winston then continued with his vivid recounting of the American epic. When the white race arrived on the Carolina coast, "they found here the savage red man, happy and free, in possession of fields, forests and streams." According to Winston, the Indian "roamed at large, a king among the beasts of the forest, but at best himself only an improved animal." Without, of course, making reference to any of the overpowering weapons brought by Europeans to North America—diseases, firearms, and liquor—Winston glibly pronounced that the Indian could not withstand the superior powers of the white race: "Before this all conquering race [white] he [the Indian] is gone and gone forever."

Next came blacks in America: "The Indian is gone. The Negro is going. The white man will survive in the fulfillment of the laws of God." Winston concluded his racial saga with an explanation of why he thought the white race was superior: "There is no room on earth today for vicious, incompetent and immoral races. White civilization is triumphant, because it is best; Christianity will rule on earth because it is a religion of love and service. The cannibal races of Africa, the idolatrous races of Asia, the savage Indian and the semi-civilized negro in America must all learn the laws of God, and fulfil them in their daily lives, or else pay the penalty of decay and final extinction." From Winston's point of view in 1908—at least as he read the Bible and history—the English race "today holds sway over the world." "There has never been another [race]," he believed, "whose expansion has been either so broad or so rapid."[14]

Sadly, there was actually nothing extreme about Winston's point of view about the eradication of Indians and the imminent decline of blacks into brutish beings—that is, from the perspective of white opinion in 1908. The most widely read newspaper across the northern coast of Carolina, the Norfolk-based *Virginian Pilot,* bristled with such allusions. On 6 February 1908, the *Pilot* reported the robbery of a white newsboy with these headlines: "Newsboy Robbed by Buck Negro" and "White Lad on Way Home with Money When Brute Stopped Him."[15] A week later, the *Pilot* reported a police capture of "eight negroes engaged in the game of skin." The arresting officers then "tied them together with a rope and marched all to the county jail."[16]

A few weeks later, the *Pilot* carried the story of how two blacks, arrested under suspicion of killing a white woman in Georgia, were lynched by a mob: "Today the negroes were taken from the county jail and carried some distance from the town, where they were hanged to a tree." Then, the story continued, "the hanging bodies were cut down and incinerated."[17] The same treatment was reported months later concerning a black man who was accused of attacking a white teenage girl in Biloxi, Mississippi.[18] To forestall similar lynchings by mobs in Concord and Stanley County, North Carolina, later in the year, local sheriffs took the precaution of moving accused blacks in the stealth of night to jails in other counties.[19]

In addition to the threat of lynching for alleged crimes, individuals with black skin or even of dark complexion often lived under fear of arrest for no crime at all. Two blacks were arrested at gunpoint, the *Pilot* reported in March 1908, when they were thought to be safe-crackers late at night in a commercial building. As it turned out, they were actually the crew that routinely cleaned those offices during evening hours.[20] Another man described in the newspaper as "a halfbreed Indian-negro" was arrested for buying whisky illegally for convicted white felons.[21] A week earlier a policeman took chase after "a negro with a crate of eggs on his back." The officer had "decided that there was something 'crooked' about the deal and called on the negro to halt." But "the fleeing negro threw grit in the blue coat's face and escaped with the 'hen fruit.'"[22]

In addition to false arrests and presumed crimes, newspapers regularly reported stories on the confusing, sometimes ludicrous efforts of a white society to enforce Jim Crow laws. In February 1908 five bishops of the African Methodist Episcopal Church filed a complaint with the Interstate Commerce Commission that they had been denied first-class seats on passenger trains traveling across North Carolina and other southern states. According to their pleading, they had bought first-class tickets for travel on these trains but had been consigned to Jim Crow cars that lacked first-class accommodations. They found the Jim Crow cars to be “dirty and filthy” and “crowded with passengers of every description or character, who smoke, drink and curse in the presence of women and all others who possess decent breeding.”[23] Further proof of the strange Jim Crow world was another incident a few months later when members of the all-white Amateur Theatrical Club in Norfolk were headed to a performance attired in blackface and minstrel garb. The conductor of a streetcar they boarded ordered them to the back row of the public conveyance. When they complied, a “respectable” black man seated there—described by the newspaper as a “darkey”—protested by leaving his own seat, proclaiming, “I aint goin’ to set by no low crap-shootin’ nigger like dem is.”[24]

The relationship between the black and white races in North Carolina had been drifting into the precarious circumstances of 1908 for many years. While black and white men still toiled together in the fishing and boating and lumbering industries of coastal Carolina, and are thus amply represented in photographic images of the period, many photographers (not including the Wrights) seemed drawn to black subjects: segregated black schools; black churches to which blacks had separated themselves; to black families gathered around rustic homes; and black children staring into the lenses of strange cameras—rarely displaying smiles.

Corydon Pirnie Cronk, who was recording the effects of hurricanes in 1899, was especially drawn to black subjects. James Hare, while chasing the Wright brothers in 1908, seemed to share a similar fascination. Their crystal-clear photographs give us indelible images of memorable black faces up and down the coast. Occasionally, other photographers, probably homegrown, also captured iconic images of blacks permanently living on the coast—usually at work but sometimes displaying their individual pride at home or at play. The all-black crew of the Pea Island Life-Saving Station, whose members were segregated from service at other stations in this rampaging Jim Crow era, was one such subject of curiosity to whites and of notable pride to black citizens along the Carolina coast circa 1903.

The Tranquil House in Manteo, gateway to history (Manteo, 1908). *The Tranquil House, on a sandy street in Manteo, was the jumping-off point to the Carolina coast by 1903 for businessmen, for pilgrims to the hallowed grounds at Fort Raleigh, or—as in the case of the Wright brothers in 1908—for another season of flying. Close to the docks on Shallowbag Bay where passenger ferries landed, the busy hostel was strategically located next to Dare County's still-new courthouse and the town's combination weather and telegraph station, providing immediate access to information from the larger world. Lantern slide, James H. Hare, 1908 (1520.642, James Hare Collection, Harry Ransom Research Center, University of Texas at Austin).*

The parlor of the Tranquil House, a history salon (Manteo, ca. 1903). *As a crossroads hostel for the banks and sounds region, the Tranquil House was a place that throbbed with fables of history—ranging from the early exploits of Sir Walter Raleigh's explorers and the Union army invasion of Roanoke Island to those storied hurricanes and nor'easters that flooded the entire town of Manteo. With memories of the Civil War nearly suppressed or forgotten by the early twentieth century, Manteo was abuzz around 1903 with a new brand of stories that romanticized the first efforts of white Englishmen to colonize North America just a few miles away and the disappearance after 1587 of Sir Walter Raleigh's last colony. Photograph, photographer unknown, ca. 1903 (AV.5205.3.110, Manteo Centennial Exhibition Photograph Collection, Outer Banks History Center, Manteo).*

The ballast stones from Raleigh's ships (Manteo, 1908). *One could neither enter nor depart the portals of the Tranquil House without being reminded of the story of Raleigh's colonization efforts. A pile of curious stones in the front yard—said to have come from Raleigh's ships—begged an explanation and provided the setting for a memorable photograph. These New York reporters in 1908 could not resist the temptation. Lantern slide, James H. Hare, 1908 (1514.636, James Hare Collection, Harry Ransom Research Center, University of Texas at Austin).*

Beasts of burden also conveyed black families to town and church (Roanoke Island, 1908). *While he was in Manteo, the photojournalist James Hare seemed to be fascinated nearly as much with the history of the region and its black residents as he was with taking pictures of the Wright brothers. On his way with other reporters to Fort Raleigh, he encountered this black family going somewhere in clothes intended for something other than work. Lantern slide, James H. Hare, 1908 (1512.634, James Hare Collection, Harry Ransom Research Center, University of Texas at Austin).*

Black workers engaged in every water-based business on the coast (Manteo, 1908). *When the New York reporters and photographers needed to get to Kill Devil Hills in 1908 or even to take a day off for fishing, they found experienced black guides (as in this picture) on many docks along the coast to provide water-taxi service or to take a group of paying customers to places where the fish might be running. The reporters shown here in Manteo that year appear to be going fishing. Lantern slide, James Hare, 1908 (1501.623, James Hare Collection, Harry Ransom Research Center, University of Texas at Austin).*

The riverboat crew of the *H. L. Myers* on the Tar River (Tarboro [?], ca. 1903). *In addition to operating their own fishing boats in the period around 1903, black and mixed-race mariners crewed the many steamboats, postal service vessels, and commercial fishing boats that plied the waters of the outer banks. In this photograph of the officers and crew probably of the Tar River steamboat* H. L. Myers, *what appear to be two white officers are shown with their black crew members. Photograph, W. A. Parvin Family, ca. 1903 (PC.5099-017, Captain Henry Clark Bridgers Jr. Collection, Outer Banks History Center, Manteo).*

Blacks found employment in commercial fishing operations (sound region, ca. 1903). *Commercial fishing was a seasonal but labor-intensive line of work. Black residents who were scattered around the Carolina coast joined in the rush from farms and other tasks to work on large fishing boats such as the one in this period image from the collection of H. H. Brimley. Photograph, photographer unknown, ca. 1903 (PhC42 Bx6F25, Brimley Photograph Collection, State Archives of North Carolina, Raleigh).*

Black and mixed-race families proudly tilled small farms (Pasquotank County, 1899). *Black and mixed-race men and teenagers—girls included—could be observed working the fertile grounds near the Dismal Swamp Canal at the headwaters of the Pasquotank River. Given this prime location adjacent to the coastal transportation systems, small-scale black farmers could also get their crops to market. Photograph, Corydon Pirnie Cronk, 1899 (AV.5138, Carol Cronk Cole Collection, Outer Banks History Center, Manteo).*

Black farmers also contributed to the timber industry (sound region, ca. 1903). *North Carolina's abundant forests around the Albemarle and Pamlico Sound regions were harvested not only commercially by large forestry companies but also log by log by black farmers working smaller stands of timber. Photograph, photographer unknown, ca. 1903 (PhC42 Bx13F13, Brimley Photograph Collection, State Archives of North Carolina, Raleigh).*

The monument at Fort Raleigh (Roanoke Island, 1899). *The most hallowed spot on the Carolina coast around 1900 was this newly minted granite monument placed by the Roanoke Colony Memorial Association in 1896 at the site believed to be the location of the abandoned "Citie of Raleigh," built by Sir Walter Raleigh's third group of explorers in 1587, later known as "the lost colony." This photograph of the still fresh monument was taken by Corydon Pirnie Cronk less than three years after the marker was installed. Photograph, Corydon Pirnie Cronk, 1899 (AV.5138, Carol Cronk Cole Collection, Outer Banks History Center, Manteo).*

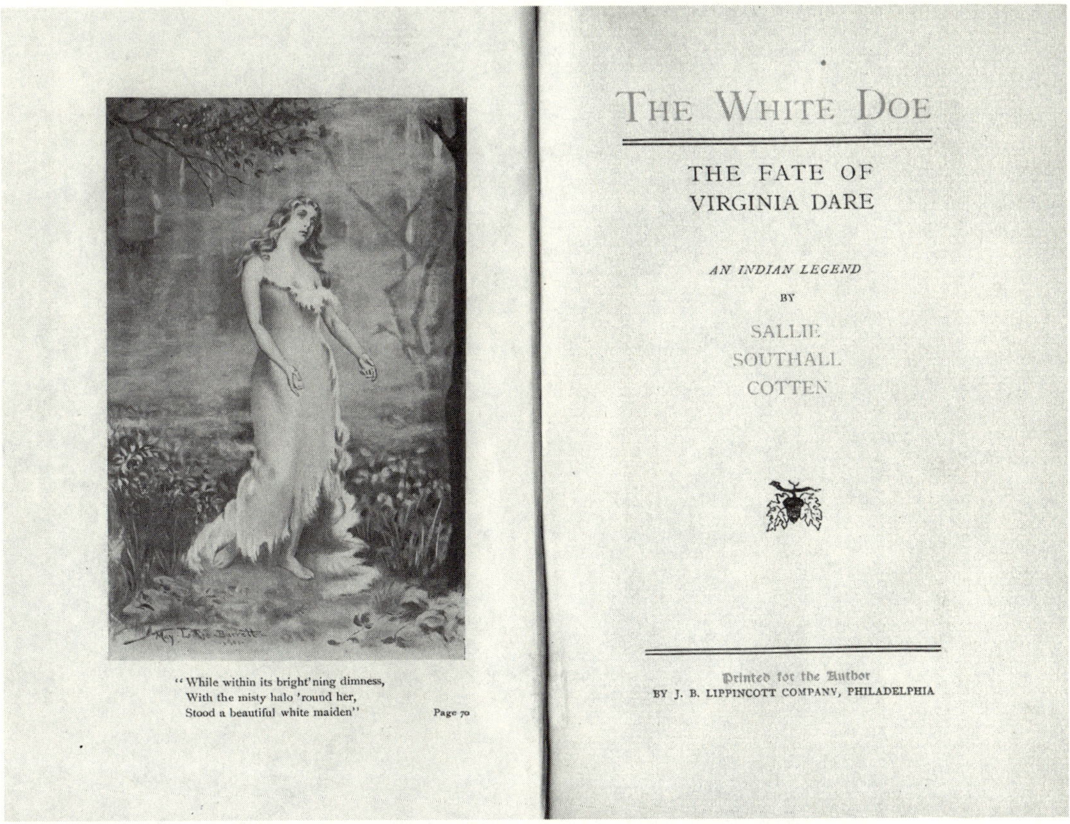
"While within its bright'ning dimness,
With the misty halo 'round her,
Stood a beautiful white maiden" Page 70

THE WHITE DOE

THE FATE OF
VIRGINIA DARE

AN INDIAN LEGEND

BY

SALLIE
SOUTHALL
COTTEN

Printed for the Author
BY J. B. LIPPINCOTT COMPANY, PHILADELPHIA

"The Legend of Virginia Dare" went forth in 1901. *Author Sallie Southall Cotten's epic poem on the transformation of the first English-born child Virginia Dare into a white doe captivated the imaginations of children and adults alike and drew wide attention to the story of Raleigh's "lost colony." Published in 1901, only five years after the placement of the Fort Raleigh monument, this romanticized depiction of the Raleigh colonies spread like wildfire across North Carolina and the nation, drawing attention to the first settlement in North America by white English Protestant men and women. Title page of* The White Doe: The Fate of Virginia Dare, an Indian Legend *(author's library).*

Reporters visit the Fort Raleigh monument in 1908. *The same big-city reporters who had their interest piqued by the ballast stone at the Tranquil House in 1908 felt compelled to make their own quiet pilgrimage to the place being described at the time as the birthplace of English America. Although sent to Manteo to report on the secret flights of the Wright brothers, they were also avid tourists. Lantern slide, James H. Hare, 1908 (1496.618, James Hare Collection, Harry Ransom Research Center, University of Texas at Austin).*

Celebrating the conquest of America by the "English race," 1908. *Inspired by romanticized stories of Raleigh's colonies and the birth of Virginia Dare, a group of Episcopalians made a pilgrimage to Roanoke Island on 20 May 1908 to commemorate her birth. Traveling from Elizabeth City to the north coast of Roanoke Island aboard the steamer* Virginia, *the pilgrims were carried ashore on shad boats (shown in the image) where "the scene was not unlike the original landing [i.e., in 1587], in appearance," declared the chronicler of the event. They trudged from water's edge to the granite marker at Fort Raleigh, where they heard Lieutenant Governor Francis Winston celebrate the conquest of the "superior" English race over both Indians and blacks in North America. Photograph, photographer unknown, 1908, in Thomas P. Noe, ed.,* Pilgrimage to Old Fort Raleigh on Roanoke Island, North Carolina, August 20, 1587–May 20, 1908 *(New Bern, NC: O. G. Dunn, 1908?), 5, 15 (North Carolina Collection, Joyner Library, East Carolina University, Greenville).*

Portrait of women in a black family (Pasquotank County, 1899). *Corydon Cronk, judging from the surviving photographs he took on his 1899 journey down the Carolina coast, was very interested in making group portraits of black families in front of their homes and of black students at their schools. In this image of women at a rustic homeplace beside the Pasquotank River, he seems to have invited the women—perhaps from a single interconnected family—to put on their best finery for this photograph. Or maybe they chose to do so themselves, while mischievous boys perched on protruding ledges of this log cabin. Photograph, Corydon Pirnie Cronk, 1899 (AV.5138, Carol Cronk Cole Collection, Outer Banks History Center, Manteo).*

A black family in front of a simple board-and-batten homeplace (Pasquotank County, 1899). *In this portrait, Corydon Cronk incorporated more details of the simple homestead. (This cabin is probably adjacent to the log cabin in the previous photograph, since it includes some of the same women and roguish boys, this time posed up front.) In addition to some of the same people, the backdrop here is of a slightly more adorned building of board-and-batten construction and glass windows. Long boards are used as roof shingles from eave to roof ridge. One of the farm's outbuildings can be seen in the background to the left; the family's pig is busy rooting for food on the right. Photograph, Corydon Pirnie Cronk, 1899 (AV.5138, Carol Cronk Cole Collection, Outer Banks History Center, Manteo).*

A North Carolina "separate but equal" public school (Pasquotank County, 1899). *Corydon Cronk seemed to take a special interest in North Carolina's declared policy of establishing separate but equal schools for black children. As he traversed northward to the first segment of the Dismal Swamp Canal, he persuaded the male teacher (third row right) at this public school in Pasquotank County to let him make a group portrait of him and his students. Photograph, Corydon Pirnie Cronk, 1899 (AV.5138, Carol Cronk Cole Collection, Outer Banks History Center, Manteo).*

Black students at a public school in Elizabeth City (Elizabeth City, 1899). *Corydon Cronk also stopped at a black school in Elizabeth City where the female teacher organized her students for this class or school portrait. Befitting this unusual opportunity to pose for a photograph, some of the girls on the last rows in the picture held snatches of roses. Photograph, Corydon Pirnie Cronk, 1899 (AV.5138, Carol Cronk Cole Collection, Outer Banks History Center, Manteo).*

Pea Island Life-Saving Station's all-black crew (Pea Island, ca. 1903). *The Pea Island Life-Saving Station, built in 1878 and located in one of the most dangerous sections of the banks, had the unique distinction in the U.S. Life-Saving Service of having an all-black crew. The station was commanded by the longtime keeper Richard Etheridge (1840–1900), a veteran of the Thirty-Sixth Infantry Regiment, U.S. Colored Troops, during the Civil War. Photograph, photographer unknown, ca. 1903 (N.77.4.29, General Negative Collection, State Archives of North Carolina, Raleigh).*

Children on the pathway from Manteo to Fort Raleigh (Roanoke Island, 1908). *The photojournalist James Hare also saw something appealing in the faces and the curious eyes of these black children as he and some colleagues traveled from Manteo to Fort Raleigh. Neither Hare nor these children would be privy to the irony that, a few days later, Lieutenant Governor Francis Winston would celebrate the conquest of America at Fort Raleigh by the white English race over Indians and blacks. Lantern slide, James H. Hare, 1908 (1516.638, James Hare Collection, Harry Ransom Research Center, University of Texas at Austin).*

6

A JAUNT AROUND THE CAROLINA COAST

On the morning of 7 April 1908, Colonel Frederick A. Olds (1853–1935), the ebullient and widely beloved founder of North Carolina's "Hall of History," departed Raleigh by train on a journey that would take him to virtually every nook and cranny of the Carolina coast. By an odd coincidence of history, on that very same day Wilbur Wright arrived by train in Elizabeth City, North Carolina. Olds began something like a triumphal tour of the North Carolina banks to celebrate how they had become an integral part of the modern commercial world. Wilbur Wright, by contrast, operating on an old illusion that he and Orville could conduct secret flights on the banks, away from the prying eyes of the world, launched into a five-week period of test flights that brought the world's press immediately to the Carolina coast precisely because it had become so fully accessible to the world.

By the time Olds finished his tour, the attention of the world had been drawn forever to Kitty Hawk and Kill Devil Hills. When the Wright brothers left these previously little-known places a few weeks later, Wilbur went directly to France where he astounded all of Europe three months later with the world's first extended powered flights in the skies over a horse racing track at Le Mans. Orville, meanwhile, captivated the attention of the American nation with his own even longer flights over Fort Myer on the outskirts of Washington, D.C.

"How many people know our coast as they ought to know it?" Olds asked rhetorically at the outset of his extended tour. "Not one in a thousand; yea, not one in ten thousand," he wrote, answering his own question. Most North Carolinians, he continued, "think of the long and slender coast line or sand barrier from Beaufort to Virginia as something quite far away and beyond them"; nor have many of them trod on "that long point of land which reaches out so far, like Hatteras, as if striving to touch the Gulf stream." The peripatetic Olds, who was also a prolific travel writer, invited the readers of North Carolina's largest-circulating daily newspaper, the *Charlotte Observer*, to go along with him through a series of articles that he titled "A Jaunt through Eastern North Carolina."[1]

Over a period of the next month, Olds took the most efficient travel routes and conveyances available at the time to observe and describe the people and places across the long and winding Carolina coastline. The first leg of his trip was by train on the old Wilmington and Weldon Railway (which by 1908 was part of the Atlantic Coast Line Railway) to the port of Wilmington. "As our train sang along the track" toward the Confederacy's last open port, Olds saw "long lines of refrigerator cars, ready for the enormous strawberry movement" northward. Along the Cape Fear River and other coastal waterways, he observed, "people up country have no idea of the enormous amounts expended by the United States in river and harbor improvements." In Cape Fear River dredging operations and in other navigation projects on the coast, he witnessed the work of "the great sandsucker, deepening the channel" and removing large stumps from the waterways, some of them "being as much as 8 feet in diameter, and weighing many tons."[2]

At Wilmington, Olds was a guest of the affable and prosperous James Sprunt, owner of the revitalized colonial-era Orton Plantation. Sprunt owned one of the few automobiles in the area and drove Olds up and down the shell-paved roads bordering the Cape Fear River. He proudly took Olds to the district offices of the U.S. Army Corps of Engineers in Wilmington to meet the powerful officer responsible for creating and maintaining the navigable waterways across the length and breadth of the Carolina coast. Captain Earl Brown, the Wilmington district engineer, gladly put Sprunt and Olds on the Corps' boat *Mercur* and took them down the mouth of the Cape Fear to Southport and Baldhead Island while exuberating about the inland waterway that was in the process of being built from the border of Virginia to South Carolina. Brown, Sprunt, and Olds shared an enthusiasm for the economic development of coastal Carolina that had infected fishermen, lumbermen, hunters, farmers, and small businessmen alike up and down the coast. Whereas some viewed postbellum Carolina as a land of spoil and waste, these individuals could only see boundless opportunity—particularly in the new partnership that had emerged between railroads, shipping companies, the federal government, and local business entrepreneurs.[3]

After getting an overview of the grand plans emanating from Wilmington for making North Carolina's coastal waters navigable, Olds began his journey toward the barrier island chain. He took a train from Wilmington to Jacksonville in Onslow County where he paused for a day of fishing in the New River. Then he proceeded, on the Atlantic Coast Line train, from Jacksonville to New Bern and from there on the old North Carolina Railroad route to Beaufort and Morehead City. "The air of prosperity is quite evident," he wrote of these places. Everywhere he heard "a lot of talk about the coming of the inland waterway and what it meant." The fever of economic development on the coast had arrived for real: "The people there seemed to realize the fact that a new era for their place is coming."[4]

After Beaufort, Olds traveled to the banks by water. Neither trains nor automobiles could traverse these territories. The first of two small gasoline boats, the *Ripple*, took him halfway to Ocracoke. At the town of Atlantic, he switched to another gasoline launch of the same size. It took a full day to ply the waters through the straits and sounds to Ocracoke Island. "Our route lay through beautiful waters and passed [past] decaying windmills which used to be so plentiful," he wrote. He and his companions saw companies of "Maryland men [who] were shipping soft crabs" in a "new and proper way." By crating them "in dry grass, which is washed up by the water, instead of in ice," the delectable crabs "will live a week and can be sent anywhere," Olds noted. "So the Marylanders have done humanity a great service," he concluded, because "a live soft crab is a delight" anywhere it could be delivered.[5]

Olds and his companions enjoyed other adventures on the way to Ocracoke. They stopped by one of the river lights in the Pamlico Sound to get a bucket of fresh water. While hooked to the iron pile, the friendly keeper surprised them by sending down a bunch of fresh bananas—which they found to be abundant up and down the banks. The sunlight was "smiting the snowy white lighthouse" at the center of the town of Ocracoke. They visited the Doxie brothers' famous factory there "where clams are made into juice or broth, which is sold all over the world." Ocracoke, like every other small town along the Carolina coast, had both a Southern Methodist and a Northern Methodist church competing with each other for tidiness and congregations. Around town, Olds noted, "the talk is all local and the State, the Mother State, seems really very far away." In speech, "the broad dialect and the old English words and phrases are really quite refreshing." At day's end, Olds climbed to the top of the squat Ocracoke Lighthouse and observed that the residents of Ocracoke and the adjacent banks villages were the only North Carolinians who had the privilege "of seeing the sun rise from and set in the water" since "there is nothing but Atlantic ocean towards the east and nothing but Pamlico sound for many a long mile towards the west."[6]

Early the next morning Olds and his companions took again to the water, headed to Hatteras in a charter boat—the only hired boat he used during his entire trip through the coastal waters. All the other legs of the trip were taken on ferries or scheduled runs of the fleet of boats that carried mail to every small hamlet along the banks. As Olds noted, "as a test we were making [our] trip through in mail boats, so as to see the ordinary methods of travel in that part of the world." Skimming across calm sound waters, Olds observed that, although the banks deprived North Carolina of any "deep-water ports," they gave "the State certain very remarkable advantages." Among these were wonderful shad and herring fisheries and "such oysters as the world loves." Observing the many river-light houses perched atop iron piles scattered around the sounds, he thought they looked "at a distance like mushrooms or water-tanks." Passing Long Shoal, a sandy lump in the sound waters, Olds watched thousands upon thousands of terns rising from and descending to their "rookeries" dispersed across the beaches. Lest one conclude that Olds was looking at an unspoiled paradise of nature, he registered a word of gratitude that his naturalist friend H. H. Brimley and the Audubon Society had fought valiantly in recent years to halt "the gentry" who "came perilously near utterly exterminating these beautiful creatures" in order "to get the feathers for woman's hats." By securing strenuous protection laws, "the State has pretty well crushed out this kind of business." Underscoring his scorn for snatching feathers from endangered birds, Olds gloried that rare terns are no longer "butchered to make feminine holiday."[7]

Olds's charter boat slid by the "picturesque" Hatteras village of "some 600 souls" and came eventually to the "cape" itself where a new wharf had just been completed with a tramway to take passengers from their boats to the shore. "The place is really subtropical," he observed, with palmettos and verdant knots of growth more common to Florida. But as he and his friends trekked on a narrow path to the Hatteras Lighthouse, he was stunned at what he saw north of the proud light. The entire landscape was a smoldering "ruin like that of Sodom and Gomorrah"! "The lumber men are at work there and the blight on one of the most beautiful landscapes of North Carolina was a fire swept place . . . and the very soil had been destroyed except the bare and ghastly sand that formed the bed for it." The entire island had been bought, and boatloads of harvested pines were being sent northward. Olds was disgusted that the local people had sold it, but, he lamented, "there seems to be very little sentiment about the matter."

Olds was well impressed by the sophisticated operation of the Cape Hatteras Lighthouse but was distressed at the condition of the lighthouse itself. It was built in 1870 to stand for the ages, but "the building is cracked from top to bottom, from north to south." A separate, smaller light known as a "Bug Light" had been positioned closer to the shore, but it had been enveloped by the sea. Although there had been successive efforts to position a floating light ship well beyond the shore on Diamond Shoals, Olds reported that "all hope of having a lighthouse out on the treacherous Cape shoals . . . has been abandoned." If these discouragements were not enough, Olds was further saddened when he looked out to sea from the observation deck atop the Cape Hatteras Light: "We also saw a fleet of 23 vessels from New York, fishing smacks, little schooners, engaged in catching blue fish by 'trolling,' each one having 67 boats which sail about, using long lines with pieces of bone called 'squids' at the end from which large hooks project." These convoys of fishing ships and their broad-sweeping methods of fishing had taken over the Carolina offshore fishing business. Despite the encroachment of sawmills and industrial-scale fishing, Olds concluded as he descended the steps of the 198-foot lighthouse, "Hatteras, like Ocracoke, is a restful place" and "to most North Carolinians it would seem really quite foreign."[8]

From Hatteras, Olds and his company traveled northward on the sound side of the banks in a gasoline-powered boat called the *Annie*—a "poor tug, at best," Olds wrote. To their delight, they were joined by a seasoned lifesaving station keeper who regaled them with stories about the dangers of Diamond Shoals and much else as their vessel plied the calm waters from one tiny settlement to another. The shoals consisted of rusty-looking hard soils and were littered throughout with the wrecks of sunken ships. But now, according to the lifesaver, "every inch of that coast is patrolled every night during ten months of the year by as fine a lot of men as ever breathed the breath of life. For them," he continued," no storm has too much terror." The impromptu guide pointed out to Olds many interesting sites on the banks, among them the many strange graveyards filled "with head stones and foot-stones of red cedar . . . so weathered by the passing years that they looked exactly like the soft brown marble and not at all like wood."[9]

Once the *Annie*'s captain struck a course across Pamlico Sound toward Roanoke Island, the boat began "making her dance like a cork" as it wove past multiple hidden shoals in the shallow sound waters. Both natives and "up-country people" onboard became seasick. The captain also cursed the "pirates" who had swept in from Virginia and beyond in the past year "stripping" the once-abundant local oyster beds. The visiting vandals took the big oysters to be canned for northern food platters and the small ones to be planted in other less fertile beds up the coast. The *Annie* next passed through miles upon miles of shad nets—"thousands of nets, long lines of them set from stake to stake, sometimes a quarter of a mile long, while others were the square kind, known as 'Dutch' or 'pound' nets." The introduction of these industrial-scale nets had produced the same effect on shad fishing in the sounds as the plundering pirates had on the oyster beds. Outside fishermen with their miles of nets had overfished the shad. These nets "literally destroy the fish, catching them all." "The big ones are sold and the little ones are prepared for fertilizer," Olds wrote. He then observed that "if the pound nets are not outlawed by the State, it will be but a few years before the [shad] fishing will be but a memory." Even as the *Annie* chugged across the sounds, it carried a cargo of boxed-up shad destined for New York. The owners of the boat annually competed for lucrative contracts to carry both shad and the U.S. mail to and from village docks up and down the banks.[10]

As the *Annie* passed through the narrow Croatan Sound and rounded Roanoke Island approaching Manteo, Olds could see the majestic sand dunes at Nags Head to his left and the historic island where Raleigh's explorers landed in the 1580s to the right. He described the dunes as "masters of everything; ceaseless, remorseless, advancing or retreating, now destroying and now uncovering what they have destroyed." As the dunes migrated, sometimes violently, he continued, "a green and luxuriant forest may be overwhelmed and left but infinitely polished and scraggy trunks." When the *Annie* entered Shallowbag Bay, the harbor for Manteo, he noted that only two county seats in the United States could be reached by boat alone—Key West, Florida, and Manteo, North Carolina. As a consequence, in Manteo, "every man has his boat, and the taxes are collected by waterways and not roads." Of the din of noise emitted by what each man called his "gasoline launch," Olds wrote, "The air resounds with the chugging of the gasoline boats, which sound like a very brisk engagement with rapid-fire guns."[11]

Once landed at Manteo, Olds made his historic pilgrimage to what Carolinians had almost always considered to be the birthplace of America. "No visit to Roanoke Island would be complete without going to old Fort Raleigh," he wrote, "and, of course, we went." Olds was there just days before the Episcopalians arrived on 20 May to commemorate the birth of Virginia Dare and to hear Lieutenant Governor Francis D. Winston celebrate the triumph of the white race in North Carolina. Olds noted that the dogwoods in full bloom gave a magical aura to the setting. Everywhere between Manteo and Fort Raleigh the dogwoods enveloped houses, "flinging their wealth of blossoms in the breeze sometimes in lines several hundred feet long." He also observed the many tall pines, noble holly trees, fine oaks, yellow jasmine, myrtles, and mounds of prickly pellitory (a thorny plant imported from the Mediterranean to make oils for treating toothaches). Despite the good work of the Roanoke Colony Memorial Association, the rail fence it had installed around the old fort site was nearly tumbled down.

Olds and his companions had the feeling of communing with another era as they looked at the fort ruins, felt the enclosure of nature, and spotted various ancient cottages in the area. The local names borne by the living or displayed on local grave markers "were very English," and "there was an air of great age with plenty of old houses with [their] queer angles." One of these was the "noted place" (or home) of Benjamin Franklin Meekins where Olds and many other travelers made a stop. Next to Meekins's home, acquired by the family in 1797, was the so-called parent vine of the scuppernong grape that had been discovered there by Raleigh's colonists in 1584–85. "Never was there a bigger fake," wrote Olds, asserting that the native grape actually came from the Scuppernong River in Tyrrell County fifty miles to the west. But Meekins himself was no fake as he proudly showed his visitors his "gigantic fowling piece, a four-bore shot gun, [with] which he had killed five swan at a shot." Meekins's next-door neighbor was "the redoubtable bear hunter Bill Basnight," who claimed to have killed four hundred bears in his fifty-year hunting career. Basnight made a pencil sketch for Olds showing how he used a "spring gun" set by a tree so that a bear would activate the trigger as it climbed the tree, thus killing itself.

On his way back to Manteo, Olds made a couple of other stops. One of them was at the Civil War headquarters of General Burnside following the capture of Roanoke Island by Union troops. "The breastworks, forts, etc., are yet quite distinct," he wrote. Another stop was at a nearly ruined windmill, one of many on coastal Carolina that had been used to grind corn into meal. At the windmill Olds encountered a man who explained island politics during the Civil War and afterward. People at the south end of the island were Republicans, he said, and those on the north end were Democrats. Those to the south celebrated the outcome of the Civil War; to the north, there were lamentations. But by 1908 residents of the island and visitors, too, were becoming much more focused on what had occurred locally three hundred years before the Civil War. That's why visitors to Roanoke Island went to Fort Raleigh when they arrived in Manteo "to start their trip." They passed by a pile of rocks at the Tranquil House said to have been "thrown out by Raleigh's colonists; stones from the old world."[12]

While at the Tranquil House, Olds surely heard that the Wright brothers had returned to Kill Devil Hills for a new round of test flights. Since the Wrights had yet to fly publicly anywhere in the world, there was great interest in knowing exactly what they had accomplished. They had not permitted any of the photographs of their 1903 flights to be published. But given that several of the lifesavers at the Kill Devil Hills Life-Saving Station had family ties in Manteo, a fertile grapevine for stories about the Wrights' activities had developed between the brothers' encampment site and Roanoke Island. The closest telegraph office in the area for the distribution of news stories was in the office of weatherman Alpheus Drinkwater—strategically located next to the Tranquil House. This corner of Manteo was thus at the moment a hotbed for the distribution of international headline stories that confirmed that the Wrights had indeed conquered the sky with their newest powered flying machine. Before Olds finished his visit to Manteo, he had thereby been exposed to the front edge of a series of news stories about the Wrights that would suddenly change the world during the remaining months of 1908. As he unfolded the story to his readers in April and May, Olds assured them that the Wrights' greatest ambition was to sell their astonishing airplane to the U.S. government—or as Olds put it—"these gentlemen are going to give your Uncle Sam the first chance, and they are right."[13]

When Olds departed Manteo, his next stop was Elizabeth City. His conveyance through "the muddy waters of the Albemarle sound" in "high winds and a rolling sea" was most appropriately a chug-a-lug workhorse of the sounds called the *Hattie Creef*. "As strange a craft as plies in any waters," wrote Olds, the clumsy boat had both a newly scavenged gasoline engine and its old sails. When the crew hoisted the "sheets" in the fierce wind, they broke loose and smashed the windows on the port side making frightened passengers "skip about in very lively fashion in the cabin dodging broken glass."[14]

Experiencing some of the stormy drama that had been observed by Wilbur Wright on his own first trip out of Elizabeth City in 1900, Olds followed the Wright brothers' usual reverse trail when they left Kitty Hawk to return to Dayton. After a brief pause in Elizabeth City to visit the editor of the local newspaper, Olds took the same Norfolk and Southern train used by the Wrights to make his own whistle stop in Norfolk. On the train, pulled by a smoky steam engine locally dubbed "Betsy," Olds noted the young crops rising from fertile soil in a section of North Carolina "where so much truck is produced." The train line between Elizabeth City and Virginia was "a great developer" because it had given local farmers, fishermen, and lumbermen access to urban markets, making Elizabeth City a commercial hub for the region.

From Olds's point of view, the bustling port city of Norfolk was "very largely a North Carolina town." According to Olds, "North Carolina push and North Carolina trade have half created it." As he went over a roll of leading businessmen and bank presidents in Norfolk, he thought "the odds are that at least half would say they were from the State [North Carolina]." Taking in as much as he could of the great naval and military complex the Norfolk area had become by 1908, Olds took a steam ferry across Hampton Roads to Old Point Comfort, the end of the train line that had first brought the Wright brothers from a landlocked Midwest to the watery realm of the Atlantic coast. At Old Point Comfort, Olds noted the behemoth Fort Monroe that had been the crucial Union bulwark in the Confederate South. But whereas the strong fort had been a scourge to the Confederacy, it had become a great symbol of unity in the recent Spanish American War. Thousands of Carolinians and men from northern states joined there with "a national spirit, broad and catholic" to board the ships of a great navy and win for the United States an empire of "world-wide possessions." Olds and his companions reveled as they took a trolley around the edges of the harbor filled with veteran battleships. He even saw the new cruiser *North Carolina* under construction in the sprawling Newport News shipyard.[15]

Having gone from Elizabeth City to Norfolk by rail, Olds decided to make the return trip by way of the oldest public transportation link between the two commercial centers—the Dismal Swamp Canal. The old canal had been long eclipsed by the much younger Albemarle and Chesapeake. But the Dismal Swamp route had recently been widened and deepened and for a brief period was conveying more traffic than its younger rival. The *Guide*, on which Olds and his friends threaded the old canal, was "a remarkably narrow and tall craft, looking like a gaunt heron." Heading up Virginia's Elizabeth River, the *Guide* entered a "tortuous creek" to the head of the canal and then "locked through" to the elevated level of the canal's path. As they edged deeper into the swampy terrain, the water looked "exactly like molasses" as the canal "went ahead along that seemingly endless ditch, with its well worn banks."

Olds observed the many small farms that lined the canal and the many horse-drawn buggies and strolling pedestrians moving along the path next to the canal. The canal boat, in fact, moved so slowly that Olds could exchange "compliments" with the "passersby" on shore. To break the monotony of the trip, Olds and his companions "had a real old-fashioned country dinner" consisting of cornmeal dumplings provided in large quantity by the *Guide*'s faithful cook "Aunt Dicey." As the boat reached the deepest-dark portions of the Dismal Swamp, Olds listened to the tales of locals who proclaimed an upsurge in the size and number of snakes and bears that inhabited the swamp. He also noticed the long stretches of cypress, juniper, and tupelo gum along the route that had not yet been raided by the lumber barons. And he examined the snarling masses of roots that made up the peat bogs between the trees. These systems of gnarled tiny roots formed an endlessly connected "sponge" that remained expanded while wet but when dried could burn slowly for days on end.

The town of South Mills, just inside the North Carolina border, was the only stop on the long journey. "There isn't a quainter place on the map," wrote Olds, as the *Guide* paused several times in the town to unload cargo at the swamp-locked village. "Nobody hurries in South Mills," he continued, since "their speed is regulated by that of the water in the canal," meaning that "nobody runs." South Mills was also the location of another lock in the Dismal Swamp Canal—the lock that lowered boats to the level of North Carolina's Pasquotank River. From there to Elizabeth City the terrain and the flora provided much more varied views. "At each bend," Olds wrote, "there was a vista ahead of us which exceeded in grace and beauty the one we had but lately looked at." The meandering banks of the river were "luxuriant with vines and tender greenery . . . and with the golden glow of the yellow jassamine [*sic*] accending [*sic*] them here and there." The glories of nature along this section of the journey, Olds concluded, "made the dull and prosy old canal seem all the more dull."[16]

Olds and his companions stayed only briefly at Elizabeth City before proceeding by train on the last leg of their coastal journey to the eighteenth-century town of Edenton. According to Olds, "old Edenton" was the "most classic place in all of North Carolina." Here, too, he was shown around the historic town by the revered blue bloods of the village. John G. Wood took him to the magnificent Hayes Plantation, the home-place of Samuel Johnston, North Carolina's most astute Revolutionary War leader. The eighty-eight-year-old Margaret Bond showed him the rich treasures of the quirky Cupola House. Others accompanied him to the town's colonial courthouse—the oldest in North Carolina—and along streets featuring the largest collection of colonial mansions in the state. On Easter Sunday (April 19), Olds attended services at Edenton's Episcopal church just as it was approaching its two hundredth anniversary. As a visiting dignitary of considerable renown and an entertaining speaker, he was invited to teach Sunday school classes for the church's children and then seated in Samuel Johnston's own pew during worship. The place was abuzz with talk about preserving the landmarks of Edenton's colonial heritage.[17]

In addition to walking through the storied halls of Edenton's historic buildings, Olds also took a day trip across the Chowan River to take a look at the grand fishery operation of the Capehart family at Avoca. Olds and a host of other visitors were taken across this corner of the Albemarle Sound on William Capehart's gas boat the *Swannanoa*. The Avoca fishery was opened by Capehart's grandfather in 1822 and had been operated continuously since that time. Describing Avoca as "the largest shad and herring fishery in the world," Olds noted the long reach of the Capehart fish-catching machinery out into the waters of Albemarle Sound. Two side-wheel steamboats entered the sound, riding side by side for two-thirds of a mile, at which point they separated and spread a net more than a mile in length across the mouths of the Chowan and Roanoke Rivers. Ropes attached to each end of the net were then connected to drums on the shore near a fish shed. Turned by steam engines, the drums rotated, pulling the ends of the net to shore collecting thousands of pounds of fish in each haul. Although the steamboats moved from dawn to dusk every day, it was not possible for them to spread and bring in the large net more than four times a day.[18]

Olds watched as one of the hauls was taken in. As the nets arrived at the fish shed, the contents were drawn onto and dumped on the wide board platform in front of the shed, leaving, Olds wrote, "a glittering mass of white, so silvery are the shad and the herring." In that particular catch, the awaiting dockside crew of twenty men, out of a total workforce of nearly one hundred employees, counted 404 shad and 20,000 herring—a small take in comparison to others of up to 6,004 shad and 188,000 herring. There followed one of the most intriguing scenes Olds had witnessed anywhere along the Carolina coast. A crew of "big black women" known as "fish wives" picked out the roe herring from the other fish "like a flash." These veteran fish cutters, "who handled their knives like surgeons, . . . gave one cut which took off the head and then a little turn of the knife and it was all ready to be washed." According to Olds, this surgery was "all done so quickly that it was hard to follow the motion." The trimmed fish were rapidly washed in vats and removed to kegs, which were immediately loaded on carts to be taken across the North Carolina countryside or to be shipped by boat and train to Philadelphia or New York, there to be consumed.[19]

This flurry of seining, hauling, harvesting, and shipping went on all day. Olds did not mention where the fishwives went when their work was done. But as for the crews of men who pulled in the long and heavy net, they were rewarded at the end of every haul with a quart of whiskey. This seemed to keep the men—an assemblage of many human colors working side by side—coming back for haul after haul all day. When the day was done, the men were plied with heavy doses of "grog" so that they were "never dry for a moment." Rendered eventually into a drunken stupor, the men piled into adjacent shacks that served as dormitories, from which they were roused the next day before dawn to take the heavy net out again.[20]

While the black women who labored in the fish houses presumably went back to their cabins and the fishing crew lay down to recover in their shacks, Olds and the other special guests gathered on the riverine beach where the Chowan and Roanoke Rivers met. There they watched a beautiful nightfall "picturesque in the extreme." "Brilliant acetyline [*sic*] gas-lights flared under the great and gloomy cavern of the fish shed," Olds noted. Across the sound waters could be seen the flickering lights of Edenton and "the lamps of different colors high up on the great transfer steamer Garrett." The genial Capehart provided for his distinguished guests a feast of food and drink appropriate to the place and the occasion. The very satisfied Olds wrote, "We were given a most toothsome supper, at the beach; of shad, just out of the water, and their roe." These fresh delicacies were supplemented with "North Carolina cornbread and concomitants." The dinner, in Olds's summation, was "indeed a feast for the gods." In thinking about his host Capehart as well as what he had seen along the Carolina coast, Olds reached one of his many conclusions about the region: "There is a largeness in this fishing life which grows upon one." As for his host, "It is no wonder that Mr. Capehart likes it. He was born to it." And so were most of the people Olds had met along the way.[21]

Olds took the Norfolk and Southern train back to Raleigh and fortuitously happened to meet Lieutenant Governor Francis Winston—who was soon on his way to make his litany of pronouncements about the supremacy of the white race on 20 May at Fort Raleigh. Olds took the chance meeting with Winston as an opportunity to talk about his trip and many other current events: "He is a man of affairs and we talked about all sort of public topics, he being well informed on all." They discussed "railway development" in eastern North Carolina. The eastern train system was "much more extensive than that in any other part of the State." And then there were the waterways: "One can go almost anywhere by water in that part of the country." The timber industry could go on forever in the rich soil of eastern North Carolina where "timber reproduces itself so fast here if it is only given a chance." Eastern North Carolina had also become the land of tobacco: "All the way to the sounds [North Carolina] has become the greatest producer in the world of bright leaf."

Olds and Winston also discussed politics and society along the coast. As Olds described the politics in places like Hatteras and Ocracoke, it was as if the people there existed in a different world. To Winston and other listening ears, Olds wrote, it was "as if we were telling of some place in the far east." On other topics such as race and labor, Olds shared with Winston and the other upper-crust whites who would soon gather at Fort Raleigh a certain blindness—as if matters of race had been swept under the rug permanently. "We were able to say," Olds reported, "that the negro question does not enter into anything in that part of North Carolina, as there are no negroes."

Forgetting—or perhaps suppressing the fact that he had just seen the efficient "fish wives" at work in Avoca and the mixed-race crews hauling in thousands upon thousands of fish—Olds reported to Winston and others what had happened to people of color along the Carolina coast: "The negroes have largely left the farms and gone to the lumber camps and they have been in great request . . . by the railways." He had also forgotten that the boats on which he traveled up and down the coast had been manned by people of color; that he had seen "a stout negro" risk his life to deliver the mail at Hog Island in the midst of a raging storm; and that almost every menial task he and his white companions expected to have done for them as they paraded by rail, by boat, and by canal barge had been provided by people of color; and that when they arrived at cozy inns, sumptuous homes, or places of feast and merriment, they were waited on by servants who were not white.

Leaving Winston with fresh observations about matters along the coast—business, transport, crops, fishing, hunting, and matters of race and culture, Olds rode the rail back to Raleigh. Winston was also duly primed to pronounce the victory of the white English race across the length and breadth of both North Carolina and the nation. According to this strange vision of the period around 1903, the supremacy of the white race in the New World had begun at Fort Raleigh and had spread from the seeds planted there to the rest of America.

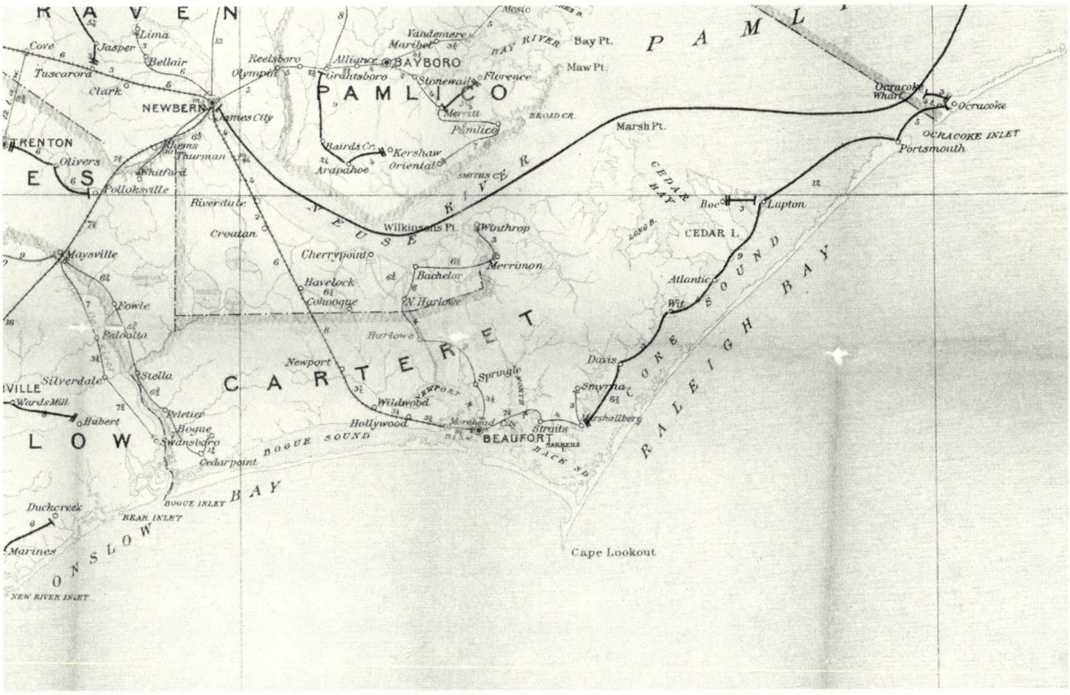

Colonel Fred Olds's route to the Carolina banks, 1899. *In 1908 Colonel Olds essentially followed the most efficient public transport route from New Bern to Ocracoke. After a brief visit to Wilmington, he took the train to New Bern, and from there to Beaufort. From Beaufort he traveled on hired boats or mail boats via the U.S. postal route straight to Ocracoke with a brief stop in Atlantic along the way. Detail of "Post Route Map of the States of North Carolina and South Carolina," 1899 (Cm912 1899u, North Carolina Maps, 993, North Carolina Collection, University of North Carolina at Chapel Hill).*

River lights served as depots for information and fresh water (Pamlico Sound, ca. 1903). *On their way to Ocracoke, Colonel Olds and his friends stopped at one of the river lights in the Pamlico Sound for information, fresh water, and a bunch of fresh bananas. When he saw the Long Shoal Light (shown here) from a distance, he thought it looked like a mushroom surrounded by rookeries for terns on the protruding shoal. Photograph, photographer unknown, ca. 1903 (AV.5169, River Lights Collection, Outer Banks History Center, Manteo).*

The squat "snowy white" Ocracoke Lighthouse (Ocracoke, ca. 1903). *When Fred Olds climbed to the top of the short Ocracoke Lighthouse in 1908, he noted that this was one of the few places in North Carolina where one could watch the sun both rise and set over water. There was nothing but water as far as one could see from the summit of the old light. Photograph, photographer unknown, ca. 1900–1910 (N.86.1.21, General Negative Collection, State Archives of North Carolina, Raleigh).*

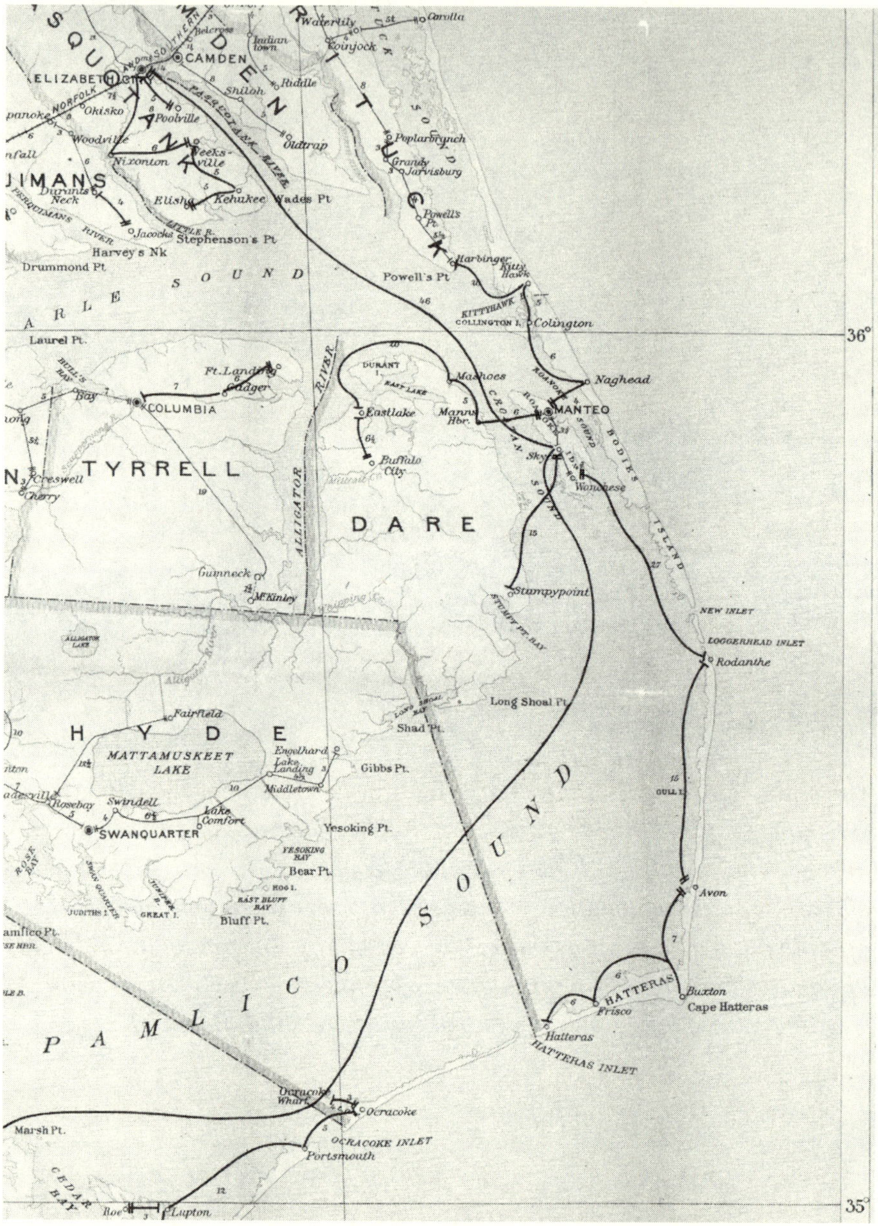

Colonel Fred Olds followed mail routes from Hatteras to Elizabeth City, 1899. *Colonel Olds observed the efficient mail system along the upper banks, including Hatteras, Buxton, Avon, and Rodanthe, as he proceeded to Manteo and Elizabeth City. Between there and Norfolk, he experimented with travel by rail, steamboat, and canal boat. Detail of "Post Route Map of the States of North Carolina and South Carolina," 1899 (Cm912 1899u, North Carolina Maps, 993, North Carolina Collection, University of North Carolina at Chapel Hill).*

The broad campus of the Cape Hatteras Lighthouse (Cape Hatteras, ca. 1903). *To the eyes of resident or visitor alike, the Cape Hatteras Light Station had all the appearance of a campus of federal government buildings—the largest symbol of national presence, security, and power on the Carolina banks. Colonel Olds found the place to be subtropical. But he was distressed that so much land had been leased to "the lumber men" who clear-cut "one of the most beautiful landscapes of North Carolina" (not distinguishable in this photograph). Photograph, photographer unknown, n.d. (AV.5125.75-006, H. H. Bamber Collection, Outer Banks History Center, Manteo).*

The Cape Hatteras Light, built for the ages, had a crack (Cape Hatteras, 1899). *Colonel Olds was also concerned that the gigantic Cape Hatteras Light, built in 1870, was "cracked from top to bottom, from north to south." The fissure noted by Olds is not visible in this crisp photograph taken by Corydon Cronk in 1899 as he assessed damage along the hurricane-torn coast. As in other places, he persuaded the keeper and some of his family to pose for a portrait in front of the imposing tallest light on the Carolina coast. Photograph, Corydon Pirnie Cronk, 1899 (AV.5138, detail, Carol Cronk Cole Collection, Outer Banks History Center, Manteo).*

One of the ill-fated lights at Diamond Shoals (Cape Hatteras/ Diamond Shoals, ca. 1903). *Olds also noted the assaults of nature on other efforts to steer mariners away from Diamond Shoals. The "Bug Light" in this photograph or its replacement was surrounded by water when Olds passed by. The last Diamond Shoals lightship had also been long-since abandoned. Photograph, photographer unknown, ca. 1903 (AV.5125.75-196, H. H. Bamber Photograph Collection, Outer Banks History Center, Manteo).*

Lifesaving station crews saved lives and told tales (Cape Hatteras, 1899). *Because lifesavers, both on shore patrols and through a telegraph system, received much information on coastal conditions and events, they were a lively source of both information and stories about shipwrecks, accidents, and heroic exploits. One such lifesaver, perhaps from the Hatteras station, kept Olds and other passengers entertained with his stories as the* Annie *headed from Hatteras to Nags Head. Corydon Cronk made this crew portrait in 1899. Photograph, Corydon Pirnie Cronk, 1899 (AV.5138, Carol Cronk Cole Collection, Outer Banks History Center, Manteo; original for N.77.4.18, General Negative Collection, State Archives of North Carolina, Raleigh).*

There were strange graveyards along the barrier islands (Chicamacomico, 1899). *According to Colonel Olds, there were many interesting and strange graveyards on the banks. They were filled with "head stones and foot-stones of red cedar" that had weathered to appear like "soft brown marble." Corydon Cronk had noted the same phenomenon in 1899 when he got a group of well-dressed locals to pose for him in and around one of these burial grounds at the town of Chicamacomico. Photograph, Corydon Pirnie Cronk, 1899 (AV.5138, Carol Cronk Cole Collection, Outer Banks History Center, Manteo).*

Despite hurricanes the U.S. Mail was delivered three days a week (Rodanthe, 1899). *Colonel Olds rode on mail boats up the sound side of the banks and noted the sometimes perilous efforts of mail carriers to get mail bags from the larger mail steamboats to shore on small skiffs. The same daring was noted nine years earlier by Corydon Cronk when he took this photograph of a black courier delivering a large sack of mail amid the wreckage left in the tiny town of Rodanthe—one of the most remote postal delivery destinations just above Hatteras. Photograph, Corydon Pirnie Cronk, 1899 (AV.5138, Carol Cronk Cole Collection, Outer Banks History Center, Manteo).*

Fort Raleigh was cloaked in dogwood, holly, and pellitory (Fort Raleigh, 1908). *Although Olds made an obligatory trek from Manteo to Fort Raleigh just a few days before the 20 May 1908 Episcopal pilgrimage to the site, he found that the place was overgrown with spring blossoms and green thickets. The picket fence surrounding the monument had fallen into disrepair. Lantern slide, James H. Hare, 1908 (1497.619, James Hare Collection, Harry Ransom Research Center, University of Texas at Austin).*

Benjamin Franklin Meekins Homestead and "Mother Vineyard" (Roanoke Island, 1908). *Both Colonel Olds and James Hare visited the historic home of Benjamin Franklin Meekins in May 1908 on their trips from Manteo to Fort Raleigh. Hare took this photograph of the 1797 property—complete with a tripod lift (foreground) for drawing water from a shallow well. Although the adjoining "Mother Vineyard" (to the right of the house) was said to be a living relic from the era of the Raleigh colonists, Olds scoffed at the idea that this was anything other than a scuppernong vine transplanted from the river of that same name in Tyrrell County. Lantern slide, James H. Hare, 1908 (1517.639, James Hare Collection, Harry Ransom Research Center, University of Texas at Austin).*

Roanoke Island contained rich truck farms and vineyards (Roanoke Island, 1901). *The rich farmlands on Roanoke Island produced an abundance of truck-farm products—potatoes, sweet potatoes, corn, pumpkins, gourds, and collards—much as they had since Indian habitation centuries before. The island was also famous for its scuppernong grapes, wine, and other grape potions from its "Mother Vineyard" vines, said to date from the first English explorations of the area in the 1580s. This heavily brushed photograph used as a book illustration shows well-dressed men picking scuppernong grapes under the carefully pruned Mother Vineyard arbor—long before the era of prohibition in the United States. Photograph, unknown photographer, 1901 (from Sallie Southall Cotten's,* The White Doe *[1901], opposite p. xiv).*

General Ambrose Burnside's U.S. Army headquarters (Roanoke Island, 1908). *When Olds went to Fort Raleigh in 1908 to participate in a new glorification of the English colonists who first settled on Roanoke Island, he still made a stop at the headquarters of the Union general who captured the island in 1862. While there, Olds noted that the ruins of the ground works from the battle "are yet quite distinct." Postcard, E. N. Anketell, 1908 (Willard Jones Postcard Collection, Outer Banks History Center, Manteo.*

Civil War politics on the Carolina coast (Roanoke Island, ca. 1903). *Between Fort Raleigh and Manteo, Olds encountered a man who explained how the Civil War wrought an enduring cleavage among citizens along the coast. Pro-Union people during the war had become Republicans; Confederate sympathizers were Democrats. Among aging veterans (such as Tom Basnight, the Union army veteran pictured here), Civil War loyalties had been replaced by matters of politics and race. Photograph, photographer unknown, n.d. (PC.5126.177, D. Victor Meekins Collection, Outer Banks History Center, Manteo).*

Hattie Creef, iconic passenger ferry of the Albemarle Sound (Elizabeth City, ca. 1903). *Built as a sailboat in 1901 with a scavenged gasoline engine added in 1903, the sixty-five-foot* Hattie Creef *was the longest-lived freight and passenger ferry between Manteo and Elizabeth City. When Olds took passage on it in 1908, both the sails and the gas engine were used in a storm with disastrous results. He thus concluded that it was "as strange a craft as plies any waters." In this photograph, the boat is near its Elizabeth City moorings. Photograph, photographer unknown, ca. 1903 (PAS 245, Photo Collections, Museum of the Albemarle, Elizabeth City).*

Low-lying Albemarle fields produced bountiful "truck" (Roanoke Island, ca. 1903). *Everywhere Olds traveled along the Carolina coast and across the sound region, he was amazed that "so much truck is produced." Along streams, sandy roads, and railroad beds, there were acres of strawberries, potatoes, okra, beans, squash, melons, and lush leafy green vegetables—such as the collards in this image—in rich cultivation to feed people near and far. Postcard, photographer unknown, ca. 1903 (Willard Jones Postcard Collection, Outer Banks History Center, Manteo).*

Waterways were being deepened and straightened (Dismal Swamp Canal, ca. 1903). *Olds observed numerous dredging and clearing operations—part of the creation of a great "Inland Waterway" from Virginia through to Beaufort, North Carolina, funded mainly by the federal government—as he headed north from Elizabeth City to Norfolk and returned up the Elizabeth River to the head of the Dismal Swamp Canal (shown here). Photograph, probably H. H. Brimley, ca. 1903 (PhC42 Bx10F3, Brimley Photograph Collection, State Archives of North Carolina, Raleigh).*

Old Dismal Swamp Canal had been widened to a thoroughfare (South Mills, ca. 1903). *The old Dismal Swamp Canal had been widened around 1900 and for a while rivaled the younger lower-lying Albemarle and Chesapeake Canal. Olds returned from a day in Norfolk via the sleeker Dismal Swamp Canal and enjoyed chatting with people along the parallel towpaths as his boat* Guide *floated by the town of South Mills, North Carolina (shown here). South Mills was one of the few stops on the long, winding canal route. Corydon Cronk had followed the same path in 1899. Photograph, Corydon Pirnie Cronk, ca. 1903 (AV.5138, Carol Cronk Cole Collection, Outer Banks History Center, Manteo).*

The “fish wives” at Capehart Fishery “handled their knives like surgeons” (Wood’s fishery near Edenton, 1899). *While on the last stop of his jaunt in the colonial town of Edenton, Olds crossed the Albemarle Sound to visit the busy Capehart Fishery at the town of Avoca. He was there spellbound by a crew of “big black women” called “fish wives” who could dissect herring and remove their roe “like a flash.” In one slash of the knife, they removed the fish’s head and with a twist had both roe and fish ready to be washed and packed. Obviously, Corydon Cronk was fascinated with the same scene when he visited the Wood’s fishery in 1899 to take this staged photograph of the women in action. Photograph, Corydon Pirnie Cronk, 1899 (AV.5138, Carol Cronk Cole Collection, Outer Banks History Center, Manteo).*

EPILOGUE

THE CAROLINA COAST, CIRCA 1903

Very shortly after Frederick Olds completed his jaunt along the Carolina coast in the spring of 1908, the intrepid scribbling traveler was ready to hit the road again. Olds had just been to Manteo and heard once again the story of Sir Walter Raleigh's efforts to colonize Roanoke Island, and his implacable interest in North Carolina's noble beginnings was rekindled to a fever pitch. For him, the Raleigh venture was a defining moment in the state's heritage. Upon visiting Fort Raleigh—"that classic spot"—he trudged over to a bluff on the eroding northern edge of the island's shore. "Standing on the crest of a sand-dune there," Olds looked across the Albemarle Sound toward North Carolina's barrier islands in the direction of England, three thousand miles beyond, and rehearsed in his mind the sense of abandonment "the deserted, lonely and terror-stricken third colony" must have felt "in the closing years of that fateful experiment at settlement which the great Knight [Raleigh] made in this State of ours." Although Olds rarely referred to Raleigh's third and last colony by the near mythical name it would assume in the twentieth century—the lost colony—he was, nevertheless, absorbed with the idea of solving the mystery of what had happened to those men, women, and children who left England to establish what they hoped would be a permanent settlement in North America.[1]

As strange as it might seem today to Carolinians and many visitors to the Carolina coast, white North Carolinians around 1903 had formed a widely shared consensus on the ultimate fate of Raleigh's last colony on Roanoke Island. Sallie Southall Cotten, who did so much to promote a national awareness of the birth and baptism of Virginia Dare, joined the unified chorus of voices when she completed her much-beloved story of *The White Doe* in 1901. In her preface to this fanciful legend of the ultimate whereabouts of the first English child born in America, she wrote: "From recent search into the subject [the fate of Raleigh's last colony] by students of history a chain of evidence has been woven from which it has come to be believed that the lost colony . . . became a part of a tribe of friendly Croatan Indians, shared their wanderings, and intermarried with them, and that their descendants are to be found to-day among the Croatan Indians of Robeson County, North Carolina."[2] Olds himself, with other politicians and pundits—and some well-educated historians—had been responsible for formulating that notion beginning in the 1880s. Not only did they create the idea out of whole cloth, but they also pushed through the North Carolina General Assembly a set of laws recognizing that among the Croatan Indians of Robeson County were to be found the legitimate descendants of the first English colonists in North Carolina. In addition to assigning the Croatans a separate legal status among white, black, and Indian residents of the state, the General Assembly also authorized the establishment of a separate Indian Normal School to educate these extraordinary people.[3]

To visit that very school was Olds's aim when he returned from his journey around the Carolina coast. In addition to having his curiosity piqued while at Manteo, Olds was also inspired by a sensational article that appeared in 1907 in the highly regarded *Appleton's Magazine* titled "The Finding of Raleigh's Lost Colony." Written by one of the better-known adventure detective authors of the period, Alexander Hume Ford (1868–1945), the article was one in a series of geographically scattered discovery stories the freelance writer prepared for the New York magazine during those years. A native of South Carolina and already an established popular writer based in New York, Ford selected a search for Raleigh's last colony as a detective thriller for his growing *Appleton's* series. By the time his lost colony article appeared in July that year, Ford was already in Hawaii learning the art of "surfboarding" alongside a new friend by the name of Jack London. Actively urged on by London, whose recent books *The Call of the Wild* (1903) and *White Fang* (1906) had given him world renown, Ford between 1907 and 1909 introduced and popularized the sport of surfing in both North Carolina and Florida on the East Coast of the United States. By simultaneously promoting surfing in Australia and New Zealand, Ford has been credited as the person most responsible for reviving the Hawaiian sport of surfing and for spreading it around much of the world.[4]

According to Ford, like so many others in the surging newspaper and magazine world, he learned about the story of the lost colonists among the Croatan Indians while on a visit to Manteo. "I first heard the tradition of the present existence of Raleigh's Lost Colony here at Manteo," he wrote. Manteo was also the starting point for a visit he made to the Croatans in late 1906. As he described his journey of discovery, he first looked at various historical documents noting the presence of "white Indians" descending from Roanoke in the writings of the Virginia settlers Christopher Newport and John Smith in 1607 and the North Carolina explorer John Lawson in 1709. Departing from Manteo just before Christmas 1906, Ford wrote, "I started to follow the trail, and throughout tidewater North Carolina met everywhere the tradition that the 'Raleigh Colony Indians' had gone either across the mainland, or by water to the great hunting grounds near the hills." "It was as an explorer that I retraced the old Indian trail across country and at last arrived among these strange people [the white Indians]," he recorded, in Robeson County. He also found evidence of their pathway in Greene and Sampson Counties which led him directly to Robeson County.[5]

Noting the remains of stone buildings, "which tradition says the Roanoke colonists taught their Indian allies to build," and also many well-kept roads ("The Croatans are still the best natural road makers in America. . . . Road building is a mania with them"), Ford wrote that he had arrived in "the most forgotten part of these United States, and among the most neglected of all the red men in America." Passing through many towns to get to the Croatan settlement known as "Scuffletown," Ford contrasted the radically different houses of blacks and Indians. "What a contrast between the negro and the Indian," he wrote. "Shiftlessness was written everywhere about the negro possessions," he continued. "On the other hand, an Indian house could be detected from afar," he noted: "Everything in repair, outhouses kept up, all the necessities for making life in the country comfortable; beehives, stables, wells, corn cribs, cider presses all in active use." Evidencing both his and what he conceived to be a Croatan condescension toward blacks, Ford observed that any Indians "who have neglected to observe the color line are compelled [by their Indian peers] to worship by themselves." This meant that these individuals "had completely lost caste by marrying among or associating with mulattoes."[6]

Ford was charmed by every Croatan he met, even though he noted that "the Croatans are uncommunicative with strangers" and "the children . . . even less communicative than their elders." He made numerous photographs of Croatans, their homes, and some of their notable activities. One of the most unusual of his published images recorded the habit of these Indians of walking single file. "I had but to look out of the window of my hotel to see the Croatans by the hundred, following each other in a single file up and down the main street of the little village, for young and old were coming to town to do their Christmas shopping," he observed. As he watched them proceed around the town "on the side-walk or in the roadway in single file," he also noted that some of them were "as dark as any Indians in America, some so light as to have red hair and blue eyes." But the Croatan had legitimate complaints about how they had been treated in North Carolina. According to Ford, "they [Croatans] consider that the whites treated them badly: at one time disfranchising them and placing them on a level with the negro." His rueful conclusion was that "they have never forgiven the insult."[7]

Ford's news-grabbing article contained no new ideas beyond the conventional wisdom in North Carolina about the whereabouts of the descendants of Raleigh's lost colony. But it displayed perhaps for the first time a set of crisp photographic images of the Croatan in their adopted homeland. And the galloping adventure tale surrounding those illustrations stole the narrative that had been emerging in North Carolina for the previous twenty years. The *Charlotte Observer* reprinted the article in its 7 July 1907 issue with an announcement that "it covers the ground thoroughly and entertainingly and North Carolinians, all, will find it of utmost interest." Among the most vocal respondents to Ford's rendition of the Croatan connection were those most responsible for unfolding the story originally. One of the responsible authors identified the other principals as the Robeson attorney Hamilton McMillan, the historian R. D. W. Connor at the University of North Carolina, the Trinity College historian Stephen B. Weeks, and the master storyteller himself—Frederick Olds. This same commentator spoke for these authors as a group by affirming, "I believe that the Croatans of Robeson County are the remnants of the composite tribe, welded from the Hatteras Indians and the English colonists of Gov. White."[8]

Spurred on by this national and international attention given to the Croatan connection in the lost colony story, Olds, as one of the original authors of this speculative story, decided to follow up his jaunt along the Carolina coast in June 1908 with his own visit to the Croatans. He wanted to replicate and expand on Ford's popular article—complete with his own photographic record. A few weeks after his return from Manteo, Olds departed by train south from Raleigh to a place in Robeson County known as Pembroke. From there he blazed his own local trail in pursuit of the Croatans. He went by wagon to a nearby settlement called Pate's—the location of the Indian Normal School. There he came face to face with more than a thousand of those same Croatan Indians who had been selected for special recognition by the North Carolina General Assembly. Standing on a wagon that served as his podium, Olds wrote, "I looked into the faces of one of the most attentive audiences possible and saw that strange blending of Indian and white." "My mind went back through the mist of years and there came the reflection that there were no stranger people on the continent than those before me." These people, thought Olds, had moved to this fertile region east of Laurinburg, North Carolina, from their prior homelands in the extreme eastern sections of North Carolina in Dare, Hyde, Beaufort, and Tyrrell Counties. The Robeson terrain made sense to him because "the lands were found as flat as a floor, with very dark soil and with streams which have all the clearness marking those which traverse the cypress and juniper region" (i.e., the Albemarle Sound area).[9]

Olds was not on some wild-goose chase when he proceeded almost directly from Roanoke Island to Robeson County. The purpose of his extended jaunt there in 1908 was to acknowledge and venerate in his own words and photographic images the presumed pedigree of these survivors of Raleigh's noble experiment. "A good proportion of them are land-owners," wrote Olds, "and as a race they are industrious." The students he encountered "ran all the way from the deep copper color of the Indian to almost a perfect white," he continued. Their homes were of a "pronounced Croatan type," being "extremely well built of logs." Despite the fact that the North Carolina Constitution of 1835 had taken away their right to vote and "made them virtually Ishmaelites," he explained, the Croatans "felt very proud of how well they had preserved themselves as a people." By comparison to the proud Croatans, Olds noted, "in the eastern part of the State the Indians have so faded a way that they are not even a memory."[10]

While celebrating the unique origins of the Croatan Indians of Robeson County, Olds sadly acknowledged that some of North Carolina's white supremacists had also taken a derogatory aim at them. "There are some people, some even in Robeson county perhaps, who speak of the Croatans as if they were negroes," wrote Olds, "but never was there anything further from the truth." Exhibiting himself some of the prejudices of the white majority of his era, Olds added, "It is a remarkable fact that extremely few [of the Croatans] show any trace of Negro taint." Cut off from both white and black populations for so many years and denied both the vote and public education, the Croatan Indians had maintained a level of social, moral, and cultural integrity that made them distinct from all other Indian peoples in eastern North Carolina.[11]

These Indians were at least in part, went the story, descendants of the all-white "English race" who had conquered the North American continent. These Indians were the direct descendants of Virginia Dare and Manteo, the principals of "the first known celebrations of a Christian sacrament [baptism] in the territory of the thirteen original United States." These holy occasions were the central events of North Carolina's glorious origins as was proclaimed by the Roanoke Colony Memorial Association on the granite monument the group had placed at the site of Fort Raleigh on Roanoke Island in 1896.[12]

Thus concluded Fred Olds's version of much the same adventure reported so superbly by Alexander Hume Ford a year earlier. Ford, albeit himself a native of South Carolina, exhibited the flawed racial astigmatism characteristic of most Americans around 1900 in his telling of the widely accepted story of what happened to Raleigh's last colony. But he did not overlay that narrative with a theory of white supremacy spun by North Carolina's reigning pundits and politicians with what they thought was the support of some of North Carolina's leading historians at its two major universities and also one of the state's most visible and active history storytellers—Frederick Olds.

As a horde of white supremacists took the reins of social and political control in North Carolina around 1900, they attempted to re-create a fictional America governed by a racially pure group of white English rulers. No blacks, no Indians, no people of mixed races, nor even women. Through the use of a body of Jim Crow laws and a black code that had evolved across the nineteenth century in both the North and the South, it was their hope to purify America. By commemorating the glorious exploits of Sir Walter Raleigh and his brave colonists and by elevating the firstborn Virginia Dare to a civil status approximating sainthood, the chimera of recovering a wholly white America proceeded. This was, of course, a similar inspiration that led these same leaders to bestow virtual knighthood during this same period on the generals and officers of the Confederate States of America—also to the unnamed Confederate soldiers who were memorialized in statues throughout the towns, villages, and parks of former Confederate states. The State Capitol grounds in Raleigh became an exhibition ground for statues memorializing the Confederate soldier, and Governor Charles B. Aycock—architect of white supremacy and segregated schools in North Carolina, as well as a monument to "Women of the Confederacy."[13]

How strange it seems in retrospect that these people who wanted to cleanse North Carolina of its black and Indian populations still had the perplexing capacity to select a group of Indians, identify them as "Croatans," and then catapult them into a starring role in their purified society.

This can only be explained by the growing racial culture of the Western world in the early years of the twentieth century and a powerful desire on the part of some Americans to identify the United States at its soul as a white Anglo-Saxon Protestant nation. This puzzling expropriation of history for commercial advantage also lay at the foot of a marketing campaign that emerged in the 1920s to make the story of Raleigh's lost colony and the exaggerated notion of the Wright brothers' first flight on 17 December 1903 the cornerstones of a program to attract millions of tourists to the Carolina coast.

The bizarre anomaly of Coastal Carolina as a surging white culture stood in sharp contrast to almost everything else that was occurring on the Carolina coast around 1900. The area had become a beehive of commercial activity through the development of a transportation and communication infrastructure that depended entirely on a mixed-race labor force to deliver rich products of the area to waiting markets. Fishing fleets, camps, and packing plants depended on both white and black muscle and skills. Timbering and lumber mills similarly employed a diverse racial mixture of axmen and sawyers who could harvest trees and deliver trainloads of rough-cut wood to builders and furniture factories. Emancipated slaves owned thousands of the small farms that provided foodstuffs—sweet potatoes, leafy greens, corn, beans, and peas—for the maws of urban dwellers. Guides white and black took hunters to freshwater lakes and sounds where wild fowl could be killed and packed for delivery up the coast as well. Although North Carolina's political leaders determined that schools, waiting rooms, toilets, trains, and trolleys would be segregated, the workplace—at least for a while yet—remained a meeting place for black, white, and mixed-race citizens.

That was the basic reality of matters on the Carolina coast in 1900. Before the next centennial moment occurred in the millennial year of 2000, public perceptions and the realities of the Carolina coast would modify dramatically. The clockwork rail, canal, and communications infrastructure of the 1900 Carolina coast would be supplanted by a world of automobiles, inland waterways, and electronic communications. Rather than being linked integrally to a larger world of destinations for the products of the region's rich natural environment, the coastal realm was symbolically and virtually turned on its head. Busy promoters—without much resistance from local residents and historians—reconceived the Carolina coast and its fragile barrier island chain as the "Outer Banks of North Carolina"—a geographic term that did not exist until the middle of the twentieth century. That was a term that made sense to people who drove cars to the coast of North Carolina to vacation but not to mariners who sailed for centuries around this vast protrusion of islands into the Atlantic Ocean.

An even more graphic term—"Graveyard of the Atlantic"—was also invented by people who observed from automobiles the remains of foundered ships rising almost as solemn grave markers in a watery horizon. That was a starkly different perception of the realm from that of mariners who saw the Carolina coast as a series of dangerous capes to be avoided, ranging from south to north as Cape Fear, Cape Lookout, Cape Hatteras, and Cape Henry. The federal government's chain of lighthouses, river lights, and lifesaving stations protecting mariners around these dangerous waters and shoals had become technologically obsolete, replaced by precise electronic reckoning. The remaining structures rising above the sea-level horizon became quaint visual reminders of another era. The former keepers of these lights and stations, hardworking technicians, were transformed through legend and literature from government functionaries into brave heroes. The old towns that dotted the Carolina coast—Edenton, Manteo, Nags Head, Ocracoke, New Bern, and Bath—saved through the dedicated efforts of preservationists—had became the locales for legends, lore, pirates, and plundered shipwrecks. In some of those towns, historic buildings were restored and some that had been lost over time, such as Tryon's Palace, were reconstructed.

All this transformation of the Carolina coast in the twentieth century largely obscures the unique world encountered by Wilbur and Orville Wright when they headed to Elizabeth City and Kitty Hawk in 1900 to study the problem of flight. By 2000 the Outer Banks of North Carolina had become a tourist mecca—a destination where one might go for surf, sun, and maybe a sporting challenge such as fishing or hang gliding (the Wrights called that kind of flying "soaring"). By 2000 one would have to search very hard to find any remnants of the magnificent transportation and communications infrastructure of 1900. Fortuitously, some of the same people who helped transform the Carolina coast into a land designed for tourists also wanted to preserve some of the natural features of the coast observed by the Wrights and others. They appealed to the same federal government that built the lighthouses to assist in creating a network of parks, wildlife refuges, and even a majestic protected Cape Hatteras National Seashore. But while they worked assiduously to protect and preserve these pockets of nature, they also called on the same national and state governments to build highways and bridges to enable automobiles to traverse that fragile and ever-changing barrier island spine. At the same time they have perpetually rattled the cages of the beleaguered U.S. Army Corps of Engineers to deepen old inlets and to rebuild shifting sandy coasts when storms and the forces of nature have wrought other inlets and rearranged sandy shores.

Another transformation that makes it difficult to understand the world of the Carolina coast around 1903 has been a thorough reimagining of North Carolina's history—especially with regard to its origins as a colony and state. Although the notion that the descendants of Sir Walter Raleigh's last colony could be found among the Croatan Indians of Robeson County (they are now proudly known as the distinctive Lumbee Indians) persisted for many years, it faced a certain doom in the twentieth century. While white supremacists and some Indians warmed to the idea that the colonists survived among a distinct Indian populace, that theory did not last among new waves of academics and researchers. These historians, anthropologists, and sociologists chose to view the close-knit community of Indians in Robeson County more as a distinct and cohesive group of Indians who withstood the vicissitudes of history rather than as an assemblage of Indians with descendants from Raleigh's lost colony.[14] By the time one of North Carolina's most prolific historians, William S. Powell, wrote a history of twentieth-century efforts to tell the story of the Roanoke colonies, his only references to the idea of a linkage between the Raleigh colonists and the Croatan Indians of Robeson County were obscured in a few footnotes.[15]

Nor did the idea comport very well with new story lines woven by those who wanted to make the Carolina coast a tourist destination. By the late 1920s, business and political leaders from Elizabeth City, Manteo, and Nags Head realized that the combined stories of Raleigh's lost colony, the Wright brothers' triumph of powered flight in 1903, and the great barrier islands beyond renamed the "Graveyard of the Atlantic"—fashioned into a single package—could become a marketing bonanza that might attract thousands of tourists to the newly named "Outer Banks" of North Carolina. There was no space in this story line to have the descendants of the lost colony located two hundred miles away from the tourist destination, nor to focus on the humble upbringing of the Wright brothers in faraway Dayton, Ohio. Their heroics in achieving a tortured notion of the world's first flight on a newly created place dubbed "the Outer Banks" of North Carolina won the day. And thus the Carolina coast of circa 1903 melted away.

All energies got directed into finding the archaeological remains of the long-forgotten Fort Raleigh where the colonists lived and the ground zero spot from which the Wright brothers launched their first powered flights. By bringing together some of the old-timers who observed the Wrights' flying experiments, they were able to determine the spot where the Wrights made history near Big Kill Devil Hill. But despite countless explorations by historians and lost colony buffs into archives and libraries and by archaeologists into the subsurface of Roanoke Island and surrounding waters where the Raleigh colonists actually lived, no viable occupation site by the twenty-first century had yet emerged. And other widespread projects ranging from Hatteras Island on the east to Chowan and Bertie Counties on the west have been similarly unsuccessful in determining what the Raleigh colonists meant when they signaled that they had departed to "Croatoan." Besides, of what use is a lost colony that has been found in a land and water environment where the business of tourism has largely replaced the rustic but busy realm that was the Carolina coast in 1903? And where a goodly part of the lure is to have the lost colony perpetually lost?

But those are stories that more properly belong to an era long after 1903.

"Slab to the Memory of Virginia Dare at Fort Raleigh, Roanoke Island" (Fort Raleigh, 1908). *The captions to this and the following photographs, except where noted, are from the original newspaper article by Fred Olds titled "Visit to the Croatan Indians,"* Charlotte Observer, *21 June 1908, 2–3, 8. While on his jaunt along the Carolina coast in 1908, Fred Olds made this photograph of the increasingly popular monument at Fort Raleigh—as white Carolinians began celebrating and romanticizing the early English settlements on the North Carolina coast. Photograph, Fred Olds, 1908 (1946.14.236a, Photo Collections, North Carolina Museum of History, Raleigh).*

The Croatans of Robeson County walked on sidewalks or roadway in single file (Robeson County, 1907). *On his journey to visit the Croatans, looking for descendants of Raleigh's "lost colony" in Robeson County in 1906, Alexander Hume Ford noted that one of their most distinctive habits was walking in single file everywhere they went. This photograph accompanied his article "The Finding of Raleigh's Lost Colony" in* Appleton's Magazine *in July 1907. Photograph, Alexander Hume Ford, 1906 (scanned from magazine).*

"The Croatan Normal School at Pates, Robeson County . . . Principal H. L. Edens and the Students of This Model School" (Robeson County, 1908). *At the Croatan Normal School, Olds encountered about seventy students bearing "tints" ranging from "the deep copper color of the Indian to almost a perfect white." He also observed that "beautiful hair and extremely fine eyes were the rule and not the exception." "The beauty of many of the girls was a subject of general comment," he concluded. Photograph, Fred Olds, 1908 (19XX.325.19a, Photo Collections, North Carolina Museum of History, Raleigh).*

"Preston Locklear and Rosette Brooks, Perfect Types of Croatans" (Robeson County, 1908). *Sharing a belief of the period that the Croatan Indians of Robeson County were descendants of Raleigh colonists, Fred Olds found among the Croatan certain individuals who he thought exhibited unmistakable European characteristics. Preston Locklear, he thought, was "a very striking type of their people." Photograph, Fred Olds, 1908 (19XX.325.21a, Photo Collections, North Carolina Museum of History, Raleigh).*

"View of a Croatan Farm House and Grounds" (Robeson County, 1908). *Preston Locklear took Olds in his horse and buggy to see a number of typical Croatan homes, including the Jacobs house, which was "extremely well built of logs with a wonderfully clean yard of shining sand [and] with abounding shrubbery and trees"—the "people being of the pronounced Croatan type." Photograph, Fred Olds, 1908 (19XX.325.25a, Photo Collections, North Carolina Museum of History, Raleigh).*

"The Cabin of Harriett Graham, Type of a Croatan Home" (Robeson County, 1908). *Olds described the home of Harriett Graham as "a cozy little cabin, with a garden adjoining, the house of logs and the furniture all hand-made, and the surroundings looking very Indian-like indeed." Describing this photograph, Olds wrote, "As guides there went with us two Croatan girls, and one of these stood up with [Preston] Locklear to be photographed." (The original caption with this picture is undoubtedly incorrect. In Olds, "Visit to the Croatan Indians," this image is labeled "Washington Lowery's Home," but, based on the text of the article, this is rather "The Cabin of Harriett Graham"; the label was subjoined to another image incorrectly.) Photograph, Fred Olds, 1908 (19XX.14.236a, Photo Collections, North Carolina Museum of History, Raleigh).*

ACKNOWLEDGMENTS

I got my first taste of the Carolina coast and North Carolina's barrier islands when my parents packed us up for one of our annual family vacations when I was about seven years old. Asking what we would see when we drove from Winston-Salem to Nags Head, my parents said there would be shipwrecks, the hangouts of pirates, and gigantic sand dunes. I thought we would be climbing on those wrecks, looking for hidden treasures of buccaneers, and scaling mountains of sand. Instead, we got roasted on hot beaches, saw no shipwrecks of any size, found no buried chests of gold, and walked out onto a lot of fishing piers where dozens of people were casting hooks to ensnare fish. I never saw anything of much interest at that age.

If ever I was to learn anything about North Carolina's ocean-jutting coastline, I needed some native guides to coach me on what that watery coast was all about. Fortunately, I have encountered quite a few people over the years who have shared with me their knowledge of and love for my native state's distinctive sounds and sandy coast. Most of this learning occurred after I began my professional career as North Carolina's state historian. As director of North Carolina's Division of Archives and History in the 1970s, I had responsibility for a far-flung system of state historic sites and museums scattered from Edenton on the north to Brunswick on the south with other places like Somerset Plantation, Historic Bath, Tryon Palace at New Bern, the battleship USS *North Carolina* at Wilmington, and the massive Fort Fisher at the mouth of the Cape Fear River. I had the good fortune of encountering the historians Herbert Paschal and Bill Still on the faculty of East Carolina University whose research and interests were the inhabitants, places, and naval vessels that plied the extensive waters of the coast. Both of them lived and breathed those coastal realms and could tell you stories about coastal life and times. Gertrude Carraway was the brilliant creator of the reconstructed Tryon Palace at New Bern and a prolific early newspaper writer and author about the upper-class culture of eastern North Carolina.

But the people who got me out into the water and transformed me from a perpetual landlubber into a historian who could begin to understand the profound and complicated environment of the coast were a cadre of dedicated folk who actually cared for specific realms of that world. They taught me that, as North Carolina's director of archives and history, I was the legal custodian of every submerged object or artifact in the state's rivers and coastal waters up to their high-water mark and extending out to the three-mile state limit into the Atlantic Ocean. They also made me aware that, as North Carolina's state historic preservation officer, I was responsible for protecting buildings, archaeological sites, and shipwrecks and any other historic property along the coast and out to the United States twelve-mile limit. Due to the fact that the USS *Monitor* was located while I was in this post forty miles off the North Carolina coast, I even found myself engaged in a terrific tug-of-war to protect that famous Civil War ironclad ship of war from salvagers and treasure hunters.

My principal educators at this stage of my development were Gordon Watts, Leslie Bright, and Richard Lawrence of North Carolina's Underwater Archaeology program located at Fort Fisher. These three individuals literally got me into deep water as we explored, recorded, and sought to protect such historic vessels as the *Monitor*, the USS *Central America*, the presumed coastal ship *Francis Waters*, and hundreds of other shipwrecks scattered along North Carolina's dangerous coast. They even put me in a small diving submersible that took me to the 220-foot resting place of the *Monitor*. In connection with our efforts to understand this hazardous and ever-changing coastline, I encountered East Carolina University's inspired geologist Stanley Riggs. Stan knows more about the configuration of our coast for thousands of years past and our very present than any other living being. He has been my constant coach on our changing coastline for almost forty years.

The renowned coastal historian David Stick and his nearby neighbor on Kitty Hawk Bay, Bill Harris, philosophically and literally carried me aloft into histories and tales of the Carolina coast. Stick wrote a dozen books about the coast and was more responsible than anyone else for creating and permanently attaching the identifying terms "Outer Banks" and "Graveyard of the Atlantic" to our state's Atlantic face. Bill Harris was the superintendent of the newfangled Outer Banks group of parks and Cape Hatteras National Seashore while I was at the Division of Archives and History. His branch of the National Park Service possessed a plane that he made available to tour me up and down the coastline for a dramatic view of the world described in this book. Bill also knew more about the people and families of the Outer Banks than probably anybody around throughout my internship as a would-be coastal historian. While writing three books on the Wright brothers, including this book in its early stages, Bill shared with me his vast knowledge of people and places around the sounds and barrier islands that were his realm.

Two people who threw me into the fray of studying and preserving vast realms of the Carolina coast were Carolista Baum and Keats Sparrow. Carolista was a gifted jewelry designer who lived in Nags Head but carried the mantle of her great aunt, the prolific author Inglis Fletcher. Like Fletcher, Carolista was a self-appointed warrior to protect the historic and natural environment of the barrier islands. She recruited me to get involved in two of her successful ventures—the creation of Jockey's Ridge State Park across the street from her jewelry shop in Nags Head and the famous Chicamacomico Lifesaving Station at Rodanthe on Hatteras Island. Meanwhile, Keats Sparrow, an omnivorous student of all cultural and historical aspects of eastern North Carolina and the longtime dean of Thomas Harriot College of Arts and Sciences at East Carolina University, recruited me to become the Wilbur and Orville Wright Distinguished Professor of History at his university in 2000. Keats and I combined forces both to celebrate the centennial of the Wright brothers first powered flight in 2003 and to promote other historic sites and events around eastern North Carolina. Our collaboration continued through a quadricentennial commemoration of Thomas Harriot's mathematical and astronomical research in 2009.

Keats introduced me to Lois Pearce Smith and lebame houston, two natives of Manteo with deep genealogical roots in two of the most important historical threads that emerged during the period addressed in this book. Lois was the granddaughter of John T. Daniels, who snapped the extraordinarily historic photo of the Wright brothers' first powered flight on 17 December 1903. Meanwhile, lebame was born into the workshop that has produced the symphonic drama *Lost Colony* from 1937 to the present. Her mother was the long-term bookkeeper and ticket master for that coastal cultural institution. Both Lois and lebame shared their deep knowledge and familial networks as I have researched many threads of the area's history and sought to preserve archival and photographic records as well as oral memories of people and events that have made this area of North Carolina unique.

Three other experts on the most dominant coastal traditions have also served as faithful guides: Darrell Collins, as historian at the Wright Brothers National Memorial, has told the story of the Wright brothers to more people than any other person alive. He has also shared with me his acute knowledge of the Indian and black heritage of Roanoke Island, for which I am very grateful. Tom Shields and Charlie Ewen, my valued colleagues in English literature and historical archaeology, respectively, at East Carolina University, have done more to track the ever-changing story of searches for the "lost colony" than anyone else for the past twenty or so years. They have also served as reliable sounding boards for many of my ideas and projects relating to the history and culture of eastern North Carolina.

When it came to researching documents, images, and artifacts relating to the Carolina coast, I have been assisted immeasurably by Sarah Downing, Tama Creef, and Stuart Parks at the Outer Banks History Center in Manteo. Their knowledge of that collection and other historical resources was invaluable in the early stages of this project. By the same token, Doug Twiddy and his son Clark of their Twiddy and Company of Duck gave me access to their growing collection of artifacts relating to the history of the Lifesaving Service in North Carolina and their equally enviable assembly of documents relating to the Wright brothers. Doug and his wife, Sharon, were solely responsible for saving the historic Kill Devil Hills Lifesaving Station on which the Wright brothers depended during each of the six years they conducted flight experiments in North Carolina. I am grateful for the Twiddys' support at the time the concept for this book emerged.

I am grateful to Rita Seelig Ayers of Shallowbag Bay for being my host and friend during most of the time this book was in development. She also explored with me some of the places described in this book, ranging from Corolla to Ocracoke. The experience of seeing these nooks and corners and spectacular sites in all kinds of weather in all seasons of the year made them come alive in a most tangible and visceral manner.

I would like to express special appreciation to two digital image experts at East Carolina University—Joseph Barricella and Laurie Godwin. Without their cordial and creative assistance, I would not have been able to manage and process all of the images in this book.

Finally, I am grateful to my sons, Larry and Nicholas, and their sons, Ben, Jake, and Ayden, for accompanying me to some of these places as well. I'll never forget how they came to my rescue when I needed to build one of my most ambitious exhibits at the Wright Brothers National Memorial in 2008. That turned out to be one of our most memorable family outings ever. Since none of them are very deep into the study of history, this was a labor of love—for which I will be forever grateful.

NOTES

PROLOGUE

1. I am grateful to a number of scholars, who have spent their careers researching these stories, for exchanging their research on the origins of these names. It appears that the now-popular terms associated with Outer Banks legend and lore were mainly the creation of a coterie of promoters who coalesced in the 1920s and 1930s to transform the region into a mecca of tourism. These folk included the Elizabeth City newspaper publisher William O. Saunders, the Manteo-based journalist and longtime Dare County sheriff Victor Meekins, and the transplanted artist and land developer Frank Stick. It was Stick's son and historian David Stick who popularized some of their creations in his two landmark books, *The Graveyard of the Atlantic* (Chapel Hill: University of North Carolina Press, 1952) and *The Outer Banks of North Carolina* (Chapel Hill: University of North Carolina Press, 1958). Among those scholars and researchers who have shared their ideas on this topic are E. Thomson Shields, Department of English, East Carolina University; Charles Ewen, Department of Anthropology, East Carolina University; William Harris, historian, Kitty Hawk, North Carolina; Michael Hill, North Carolina Office of Archives and History, Raleigh; lebame houston, historian, Roanoke Island Historical Association, Manteo, North Carolina; Robert Anthony, North Carolina Collection, Wilson Library, University of North Carolina at Chapel Hill; and Nicholas Graham, North Carolina Maps Project, Wilson Library, University of North Carolina at Chapel Hill. For more information, particularly on the emergence of the term "Lost Colony," see Larry E. Tise, "'The Lost Colony Film': A Mixed Message of Violence and Peace," *North Carolina Literary Review* 21 (2012): 12–28.

2. One of the most delightful letters in all the Wright brothers' papers is a letter of 29 September 1902 in which Orville Wright made much fun of a French author's efforts to describe the feelings of a bird while it was flying: "I didn't take much stock in that story, anyway, as the author probably knew less about the emotions of a bird than I, he very likely never having been off the ground on wings! In this line—that of flying—

I am now making great claims." Orville Wright to Katharine Wright, 29 September 1902, Wilbur and Orville Wright Papers, Library of Congress.

3. This is the wording on the label that the estate of Orville Wright stipulated must be exhibited with the brothers' 1903 Kitty Hawk Flyer when it was transferred in 1948 from the estate to the Smithsonian Institution, as explained by Tom D. Crouch, *The Bishop's Boys: A Life of Wilbur and Orville Wright* (New York: W. W. Norton, 1989), 526–29.

4. The best listing of all known experimental flights by the Wright brothers and Orville's description of the 17 December 1903 flight appear in Arthur G. Renstrom, *Wilbur and Orville Wright: A Chronology* (Washington, DC: Library of Congress, 1975), 126–39, 151–52, 199–202.

5. Biographical data on Corydon Pirnie Cronk was provided by his granddaughter Carol Cronk Cole of Terrace Park, Ohio, December 2014. Mrs. Cole permitted the Outer Banks History Center to scan Cronk's 1899 photographs.

6. For biographical data see Marcus B. Simpson, "Herbert H. Brimley," in *Dictionary of North Carolina Biography*, ed. William S. Powell (Chapel Hill: University of North Carolina Press, 1979), 1:228.

7. For biographical data see Beth D. Crabtree, "Frederick A. Olds," in Powell, *Dictionary of North Carolina Biography*, 4:392–93.

8. For biographical data see David Stick, "Daniel Victor Meekins," in Powell, *Dictionary of North Carolina Biography*, 4:248.

9. For more information on the Wright brothers' large collections of photographs at both the Library of Congress and Wright State University, Dayton, Ohio, see Larry E. Tise, *Hidden Images: Discovering Details in the Wright Brothers' Kitty Hawk Photographs, 1900–1911* (Charleston: History Press, 2005). Biographical data on Lorin Wright was compiled from various sources, including Bishop Milton Wright, *Diaries, 1857–1917* (Dayton, OH: Wright State University Libraries, 1999).

10. Compiled from the author's files of collected data on both George A. Spratt and John T. Daniels.

11. For a detailed history of both the Wrights' sequestration of their photographs and the race among photographers to secure images of their flights, see Larry E. Tise, *Conquering the Sky: The Secret Flights of the Wright Brothers at Kitty Hawk* (New York: Palgrave Macmillan, 2009).

12. Compiled from Lewis L. Gould and Richard Greffe, *Photojournalist: The Career of Jimmy Hare* (Austin: University of Texas Press, 1977).

13. Compiled from the author's research notes of conversations with relatives of Van Ness Harwood and from the Van Ness Harwood Collection the relatives donated to Joyner Library, East Carolina University, Greenville.

14. W. C. Kerr, "North Carolina," in *Encyclopedia Britannica*, 9th ed., American reprint (Philadelphia: J. M. Stoddart, 1884), 17:572–76.

15. Ibid., 572–75 and plate 18, between 572 and 573. "A New Map of North Carolina, 1894," from the *Rand McNally Atlas* (New York: Rand McNally, 1894), may be found in North Carolina Maps, 614, North Carolina Collection, University of North Carolina at Chapel Hill.

CHAPTER 1

1. Wilbur Wright to Milton Wright, 9 September 1900, Wilbur and Orville Wright Papers, Library of Congress (hereafter Wright Papers, Library of Congress).

2. Octave Chanute to Wilbur Wright, 17 May 1900, and Joseph J. Dosher to Wilbur Wright, 16 August 1900, Wright Papers, Library of Congress.

3. Memorandum, Wilbur Wright, 13 September 1900, Wright Papers, Library of Congress.

4. Wilbur Wright to Milton Wright, 23 September 1900, Wright Papers, Library of Congress.

5. Wilbur Wright to Milton Wright, 23 September 1900, and Orville Wright to Katharine Wright, 14 October 1900, Wright Papers, Library of Congress.

6. Orville Wright to Katharine Wright, 14 October 1900, Wright Papers, Library of Congress.

7. Orville Wright to Katharine Wright, 18 October 1900, Wright Papers, Library of Congress.

8. Orville Wright to Katharine Wright, 14 October 1900, Wright Papers, Library of Congress.

9. Collier Cobb, "Where the Wind Does the Work," *National Geographic Magazine* 17, no. 6 (June 1906): 6, 310, 313–14. Cobb's explanation of change on the banks reflected pretty much the conventional wisdom of local residents until scientists had computers that could process the large body of data accumulated annually by the National Oceanic and Atmospheric Administration (NOAA) and the National Aeronautics and Space Administration (NASA) during the second half of the twentieth century. Much of this data is summarized and explained in *The Battle for North Carolina's Coast*, coauthored by Stanley R. Riggs, Dorothea V. Ames, Stephen J. Culver, and David J. Mallinson (Chapel Hill: University of North Carolina Press, 2011). Many years earlier, the renowned banks historian David Stick had addressed this same topic in his classic work *The Outer Banks of North Carolina, 1584–1958* (Chapel Hill: University of North Carolina Press, 1958). Riggs and his colleague Dorothea V. Ames have also addressed the complexity of North Carolina's changing coastal environment in an important essay titled "An Uncompromising Environment: North Carolina's 'Land of Water' Coastal System," in *New Voyages to Carolina: Reinterpreting North Carolina History*, ed. Larry E. Tise and Jeffrey J. Crow (Chapel Hill: University of North Carolina Press, 2017), 14–40.

10. Gary S. Dunbar, *Historical Geography of the North Carolina Outer Banks* (Baton Rouge: Louisiana University Press, 1958), 218, plate 7, "Historic Inlets."

11. Ibid., 26–29, 46–51.

12. Francis Winslow, *Report on the Waters of North Carolina, with Reference to the Cultivation of Oysters, together with the Results of the Survey of Oyster Beds* (Raleigh: North Carolina Department of Agriculture, 1887), 3–4. However, Winslow noted that the 5.6 billion tons of fresh water in the Albemarle River pouring into the Pamlico Sound as its only outlet to the Atlantic affected all aspects of maritime life and culture along the inner parts of the Outer Banks. The abundance of freshwater fish in the Albemarle was noted by Frank Vaughan, *The Albemarle District of North Carolina* (Elizabeth City, NC, 1895), 9–10.

13. Ibid.

14. Wilbur Wright to Katharine Wright, 23 October 1900, Wright Papers, Library of Congress.

CHAPTER 2

1. On Israel Perry, see Wilbur Wright to Milton Wright, 13 September 1900, and Orville Wright to Katharine Wright, 14 October 1900, Wilbur and Orville Wright Papers, Library of Congress (hereafter Wright Papers, Library of Congress). On Captain Midgett and his sons Truxton and Spencer, see especially Orville Wright Diary, 27 August, 1, 8, 13, 15, 23 October 1902; 8 October, 16, 20 November 1903; and 10, 13, 15, 17, 18, 20 April 1908, Wright Papers, Library of Congress.

2. The many efforts to link coastal Carolina to the Chesapeake region are described in Alexander Crosby Brown, *Juniper Waterway: A History of the Albemarle and Chesapeake Canal* (Charlottesville: University Press of Virginia, 1981), 8–17.

3. Ibid., 43–44, 56–60.

4. Ibid., 124–30.

5. Ibid., 135–36.

6. Fred A. Olds, "The Great Inland Waterway," *Charlotte Observer*, 31 May 1908, sec. 2, p. 3; Richard V. Spell, "John Humphrey Small," in *Dictionary of North Carolina Biography*, ed. William S. Powell (Chapel Hill: University of North Carolina Press, 1979), 5:366.

7. These figures are published on the website of the American Automobile Association, http://newsroom.aaa.com/about-aaa/history/ (accessed 16 December 2013).

8. Wilbur Wright to [Family], 13 September 1900, Wright Papers, Library of Congress.

9. Orville Wright Diary, 23–25 September 1903, Wright Papers, Library of Congress.

10. Frank Vaughan, *The Albemarle District of North Carolina* (Elizabeth City, NC, 1895), 7–8, 18–19.

CHAPTER 3

1. Wilbur Wright to [Family], 13 September 1900, Wilbur and Orville Wright Papers, Library of Congress (hereafter Wright Papers, Library of Congress).

2. Russ Rowlett, *The Light House Directory*, http://www.unc.edu/~rowlett/lighthouse/ (accessed 10 January 2014). The Rowlett *Light House Directory* is a magnificent guide to more than 17,000 lighthouses around the world.

3. Ray Jones, *The Lighthouse Encyclopedia* (Guilford, CT: Globe Pequot Press, 2004), 19–25, 66–67.

4. Compiled from *Southeast Lighthouses: Illustrated Map and Guide* (Rhinebeck, NY: BellaTerra Maps, 2010).

5. See United States Light-House Establishment, *Instructions to Light-Keepers and Masters of Light-House Vessels, 1902* (Washington, DC: Government Printing Office, 1902), noting, particularly, the requirements to be courteous at all times, avoid intoxication, wear uniforms, observe local game laws, keep journals and business records, maintain a constant painting schedule, and participate in emergency operations (5–8, 12, 15, 17, 50–55).

6. Joseph J. Dosher to Wilbur Wright, 16 August 1900, Wright Papers, Library of Congress.

7. Ralph Shanks, Wick York, and Lisa Woo Shanks, eds., *The U.S. Life-Saving Service: Heroes, Rescues and Architecture of the Early Coast Guard* (Petaluma, CA: Costaño Books, 1996), 7–11.

8. Shanks, York, and Shanks, *U.S. Life-Saving Service*, 13–15; Kathleen A. Foster, *Shipwreck!: Winslow Homer and "The Life Line"* (Philadelphia: Philadelphia Museum of Art, 2012), 45–53.

9. Joe A. Mobley, *Ship Ashore!: The U.S. Lifesavers of Coastal North Carolina* (Raleigh: North Carolina Division of Archives and History, 1994), 53–75.

10. Jay Barnes, *North Carolina's Hurricane History*, 3rd ed. (Chapel Hill: University of North Carolina Press, 2001), 42–46, 49–61.

CHAPTER 4

1. Joseph J. Dosher, Kitty Hawk Weather Station, to Wilbur Wright, 16 August 1900; William J. Tate to Wilbur Wright, 18 August 1900; and Memorandum, Wilbur Wright, 13 September 1900; in Wilbur and Orville Wright Papers, Library of Congress (hereafter Wright Papers, Library of Congress.

2. Receipt, Cumpston Goffigon, James E. Etheridge and Co., to Wilbur Wright, 18 September 1900; and Wilbur Wright to Milton Wright, 23 September 1900, Wright Papers, Library of Congress.

3. Orville Wright to Katharine Wright, 14 October 1900, Wright Papers, Library of Congress.

4. Frank Vaughan, *The Albemarle District of North Carolina* (Elizabeth City, NC, 1895), 8–10, 12–14.

5. W. Kcats Sparrow, "George Higby Throop," in *Dictionary of North Carolina Biography*, ed. William S. Powell (Chapel Hill: University of North Carolina Press, 1979), 6:33; Richard Walser, "The Mysterious Case of George Higby Throop (1818–1896)," *North Carolina Historical Review* 33, no. 1 (January 1956): 12–44.

6. Catherine W. Bisher, *The "Unpainted Aristocracy": The Beach Cottages of Old Nags Head* (Raleigh: North Carolina Division of Archives and History, 1992), 10–20.

7. Orville Wright to Katharine Wright, 23 October 1902, Wright Papers, Library of Congress.

8. Orville Wright to Katharine Wright, 14 October 1900, Wright Papers, Library of Congress.

9. Alexander Hunter, "The Club-Houses of Currituck Sound," *Harper's Weekly*, 12 March 1892, 253–55.

CHAPTER 5

1. For an illuminating depiction of the omnipresence of black and mixed-race boatmen across eastern North Carolina, see David Cecelski, *The Waterman's Song: Slavery and Freedom in Maritime North Carolina* (Chapel Hill: University of North Carolina Press, 2001), 25–56, 153–78.

2. The story of the Roanoke Island Freedmen's Colony is told in detail by Patricia C. Click, *Time Full of Trial: The Roanoke Island Freedmen's Colony, 1862–1867* (Chapel Hill: University of North Carolina Press, 2001).

3. The recasting of the Wilmington riots of 1898 was accomplished through a variety

of studies and reports inspired by a pioneering book by H. Leon Prather, *We Have Taken a City: The Wilmington Racial Massacre and Coup of 1898* (Cranbury, NJ: Associated University Presses, 1984), and especially by an impassioned group of essays that appeared in *Democracy Betrayed: The Wilmington Race Riot of 1898 and Its Legacy*, ed. David S. Cecelski and Timothy Tyson (Chapel Hill: University of North Carolina Press, 1998).

4. The status of blacks in Dayton, Ohio, and in the Wright family is detailed by Edward J. Roach, *The Wright Company from Invention to Industry* (Athens: Ohio University Press, 2014), 9–12.

5. Orville Wright Diary, 15 October 1902, Wilbur and Orville Wright Papers, Library of Congress (hereafter Wright Papers, Library of Congress).

6. When they finally arrived at Kill Devil Hills, they found that their tools and lumber and other materials had already been shipped to Kitty Hawk and had not been affected by the Elizabeth City station fire. Orville Wright to Katharine Wright, 26 September 1903, Wright Papers, Library of Congress. Wilbur almost surely encountered the story of Raleigh's settlements on Roanoke Island again in 1908 when a small army of reporters who had spied on the brothers' secret flights at Kill Devil Hills in May that year were departing the Tranquil House to visit the site of Fort Raleigh and a group of two hundred Episcopal pilgrims on their way to Fort Raleigh were due to arrive momentarily in Manteo. On the brothers' various observations on the Raleigh colonies, see Larry E. Tise, "The Wright Brothers and the Lost Colony," in *Lost Colony 2005 Souvenir Program* (Manteo: Roanoke Island Historical Association, 2005), 14.

7. The many careers and considerable successes of Johnson are outlined in Willard B. Gatewood Jr., "Edward A. Johnson," *Dictionary of North Carolina Biography*, ed. William S. Powell (Chapel Hill: University of North Carolina Press, 1979), 3:288–89. Convinced that there was no possibility of overcoming white supremacist controls in North Carolina, Johnson moved to the Harlem district of New York City in 1907. There, he was elected many times to the New York General Assembly, securing the passage of laws giving blacks access to New York social services; he also played a major role in paving the way for the black-driven cultural awakening known as the Harlem Renaissance.

8. Airships—in contrast to airplanes—were held aloft by a gas, usually hydrogen or helium, that was lighter than air. Airplanes were, of course, carried aloft and remained in flight by an air foil that produced lift when pushed, usually by a powered engine and propellers, into a stream of air. At the same time the Wrights were experimenting with air foils, German engineers were perfecting a line of airships known as Zeppelins (after their designer) that were far advanced beyond any similar craft being built in the rest of Europe or America.

9. E. A. Johnson, *Light Ahead for the Negro* (New York: Grafton Press, 1904), 1–12, 120–32. H. G. Wells, *War in the Air* was originally published with lavish illustrations in 1907 in *Pall Mall Magazine*. It was subsequently issued as an illustrated book in 1908 by the London publisher George Bell and Sons.

10. Neil Fulghum, "Francis D. Winston," in Powell, *Dictionary of North Carolina Biography*, 6:244–45.

11. William S. Powell, *Paradise Preserved* (Chapel Hill: University of North Carolina

Press, 1965), 52–61, 78–82; Sallie Southall Cotten, *The White Doe: The Fate of Virginia Dare, an Indian Legend* (Philadelphia: J. B. Lippincott, 1901).

12. Thomas P. Noe, ed., *Pilgrimage to Old Fort Raleigh on Roanoke Island, North Carolina, August 20, 1587–May 20, 1908* [New Bern, NC: O. G. Dunn, 1908?]. This curious and rare forty-one-page pamphlet contains all the proceedings of this religious venture, a few very blurry photographs, and some amateurish drawings of the trip.

13. Francis D. Winston, "Roanoke Island Oration," in Noe, *Pilgrimage to Old Fort Raleigh*, 21–40.

14. Ibid., 21, 37.

15. "Newsboy Robbed by Buck Negro," *Virginian Pilot*, 6 February 1908.

16. "Negroes Marched to Jail Tied Together," *Virginian Pilot*, 14 February 1908.

17. "Negroes Lynched, Bodies Burned, in Georgia," *Virginian Pilot*, 6 March 1908.

18. "Mob Takes Negro from Jail and Lynch Him," *Virginian Pilot*, 11 November 1908.

19. "Mob's Vengeance Was Defeated in Carolina," *Virginian Pilot*, 15 October 1908; "White Woman Is Assaulted; Fears of Lynching," *Virginian Pilot*, 16 December 1908.

20. "Patrolmen Capture Negroes in Office," *Virginian Pilot*, 4 March 1908.

21. "Negro Bought Liquor for Men on the List," *Virginian Pilot*, 21 May 1908.

22. "He Lost the Negro but Secured the Eggs," *Virginian Pilot*, 6 May 1908.

23. "Colored Bishops Make High Kick on 'Jim-Crow,'" *Virginian Pilot*, 27 February 1908.

24. "Negro Minstrels Put on 'Jim-Crow' Seats," *Virginian Pilot*, 30 April 1908.

CHAPTER 6

1. Frederick A. Olds provided six articles in this series with the joint title "A Jaunt through Eastern North Carolina" to the *Charlotte Observer* for publication in its Sunday feature section. The articles appeared on 3, 10, 17, 24, and 31 May, with the last on 7 June 1908. A seventh article—which was a virtual epilogue to the series—appeared on 21 June 1908 with the title "A Visit to the Croatan Indians." The articles uniformly appeared in the features section and were usually confined to a single but very ample page. Only the seventh article included photographs taken either by Olds or by an unnamed traveling companion who he identified only as "an artist was along, not with pencil, but with the truer camera, to fix impressions forever."

2. Olds, "Jaunt through Eastern North Carolina: First Letter," *Charlotte Observer*, 3 May 1908, sec. 2, p. 5.

3. Ibid.

4. Olds, "A Jaunt through Eastern North Carolina: Second Letter," *Charlotte Observer*, 10 May 1908, sec. 2, p. 3.

5. Ibid.

6. Ibid.

7. Ibid.

8. Ibid.

9. Olds, "A Jaunt through Eastern North Carolina: Fourth Letter," *Charlotte Observer*, 24 May 1908, sec. 2, p. 6.

10. Ibid.

11. Ibid. Olds mistakenly identified Key West as being in Texas—an odd error for one so cosmopolitan as he was.

12. Ibid.

13. Olds, "A Jaunt through Eastern North Carolina: Fifth Letter," *Charlotte Observer*, 31 May 1908, sec. 2, p. 3. Olds does not make clear whether he actually crossed over the Croatan Sound to visit the Wright camp at Kill Devil Hills.

14. Ibid.

15. Ibid.

16. Ibid.

17. Ibid. and Olds, "A Jaunt through Eastern North Carolina: Sixth Letter," *Charlotte Observer*, 7 June 1908, sec. 2, p. 2.

18. Olds, "Sixth Letter," sec. 2, p. 2.

19. Ibid.

20. Ibid.

21. Ibid.

EPILOGUE

1. Frederick A. Olds, "A Visit to the Croatan Indians," *Charlotte Observer*, 21 June 1908, sec. 2, pp. 2–4.

2. Sallie Southall Cotten, *The White Doe: The Fate of Virginia Dare, an Indian Legend* (Philadelphia: J. B. Lippincott, 1901), 13.

3. Robin Purser Stacy, "Hamilton McMillan," in *Dictionary of North Carolina Biography*, ed. William S. Powell (Chapel Hill: University of North Carolina Press, 1979), 4:175. See also Stephen B. Weeks, "The Lost Colony of Roanoke: Its Fate and Survival," *Papers of the American Historical Association* 5 (October 1891): 107–46; and H. G. Jones, "Stephen Beauregard Weeks," in Powell, *Dictionary of North Carolina Biography*, 6:152–53.

4. Malcolm Gault-Williams, "Alexander Hume Ford (1868–1945)," 2–7, 15–16, Legendary Surfers.com, http://legendarysurfers.com/blog/ahford.doc.pdf (accessed 30 January 2018). This surfer biography is based heavily on Valerie V. Noble, *Hawaiian Prophet: Alexander Hume Ford* (Smithtown, N.Y.: Exposition Press, 1980).

5. Alexander Hume Ford, "The Finding of Raleigh's Lost Colony," *Appleton's Magazine*, July 1907, 22–25.

6. Ibid., 28–29.

7. Ibid., 26–27.

8. "The Sunday Observer," *Charlotte Observer*, 6 July 1907, 4. J. H. M, "For the Messenger," *Wilmington Messenger*, 14 July 1907, 6. This article was printed in a similar form in the *Charlotte Observer* on 21 July 1907, 12, and in the *Robesonian* (Lumberton) on 25 July 1907, 3. Exactly one month later, the first article on Ford's adventures while surfing in Hawaii was reported as "Alexander Hume Ford, a Writer of Sports," *Charlotte Observer*, 25 August 1907, 15.

9. Olds, "Visit to the Croatan Indians," 2.

10. Ibid. Here, Olds was referring to a reservation that had been created by the North Carolina colonial assembly in Bertie County for those Tuscarora groups that had collaborated with North Carolina during the Tuscarora War of 1711–15. This was

only one of the many Indian reservations that had been created for Indian nations that had been displaced from their lands by land-hungry European colonists. At various points in the colonial era, reservations had been created for the Weapomeoc, Core, Mattamuskeet, Chowan, and other Indian nations. But all of these had largely disappeared by the early nineteenth century.

11. Olds, "Visit to the Croatan Indians," 2.

12. Much of this information—though not the perspective described here—is outlined in William S. Powell, *Paradise Preserved: A History of the Roanoke Island Historical Association* (Chapel Hill: University of North Carolina Press, 1965), 79–82.

13. Catherine Bishir, "Landmarks of Power: Building a Southern Past, 1885-1915," *Southern Cultures* (1993): 5–45.

14. Malinda Maynor Lowery, in her book *Lumbee Indians in the Jim Crow South: Race, Identity, and the Making of a Nation* (Chapel Hill: University of North Carolina Press, 2010), describes the complex challenges faced by the Indians of Robeson County in a period when both the nations of Europe and the United States were pursuing a variety of scientific schemes for determining racial mixture and purity. Lowery has expanded her history of the Lumbee Indians' travail in *The Lumbee Indians: An American Struggle* (Chapel Hill: University of North Carolina Press, 2018).

15. Powell, *Paradise Preserved*, is a superb history not only of the Roanoke Island Historical Association but also of many anterior efforts and organizations that sprang up at the end of the nineteenth century to preserve Fort Raleigh, to interpret the history of the Roanoke colonies, and to launch Paul Green's magnificent and pioneering outdoor drama, *The Lost Colony*. While Powell (who remained an advocate of efforts to explore Fort Raleigh and the Roanoke story until his health failed in the early 2000s) referred to a presentation Stephen Weeks had made at the American Historical Association in 1890, he discounted those parts of Weeks's paper devoted "to the tradition that Indians were later discovered who claimed descent from the Lost Colonists" (31). He also made reference to discussions he had with the great chronicler of the Roanoke ventures David Beer Quinn in the 1950s on the cadre of "galley slaves and a few soldiers (all mainly Moors), Negro domestic slaves, and several hundred South American Indians" that Sir Francis Drake brought with him to Roanoke Island in 1586. It was Quinn's opinion, Powell reported, that Drake took the Moors back to England to be used in negotiations with Spanish diplomats. With regard to "the Negroes" and the South American Indians, Quinn thought that they might have been put ashore or drowned at sea. Powell then added, "If put ashore it is possible, he [Quinn] stated, that they account for the Negroid features observed among the 'Croatan Indians' of Robeson County at a later date" (7n). Powell also mentioned the second speech made by former lieutenant governor Francis Winston at Fort Raleigh in 1915, summarizing that Winston "offered a review of the claims expressed earlier by Hamilton McMillan and Stephen B. Weeks that the Croatan Indians (now called Lumbee Indians) of Robeson County were descendants of the Lost Colonists" (87). At least this was Powell's surmise, since the article from the *Raleigh News and Observer* (20 August 1915, 8), makes no reference to McMillan or Weeks and seems to indicate that Winston presented the Raleigh-Croatan linkage as his own story.

INDEX OF MEDIA FORMATS

The images included in this book are digital scans derived from a variety of precious historical media formats. Most of the images are scans of photographic prints. However, many of the other images were captured from other media requiring intermediate transfer to positive images. As a guide to readers interested in these media formats the following is a page reference to each type.

GENERAL INDEX

Page numbers in italics refer to illustrations and illustration captions.

ABOUT THE AUTHOR

Larry E. Tise grew up in Winston-Salem, North Carolina, about three hundred miles and more than six hours of hard driving to the Carolina coast where Wilbur and Orville Wright invented flight. On family vacations to the Wright Memorial at Kill Devil Hills and to the old brick Smithsonian Museum in Washington, D.C., he heard the inspiring Wright brothers' story.

Though many kids stood in awe of the ambitious aeronauts from Ohio, Tise was puzzled to learn that the Wrights' original Kitty Hawk Flyer of 1903 did not arrive at the Smithsonian until 1948. Only then did America's national museum stop pretending that its former secretary Samuel P. Langley preceded the Wrights in building the world's first powered machine capable of flight.

Tise helped organize the seventy-fifth anniversary of the Wrights' historic 1903 flight as director of North Carolina's Division of Archives and History in 1978. He cared for the brothers' historic air foils at Philadelphia's Franklin Institute in the 1990s. When he became a Faculty Fellow at NASA's Langley Research Center in 2000, he began researching the physical environment where the Wrights conducted their pioneering flight experiments. He discovered that the Carolina coastal clime was far different from what the Wrights expected. Nor did it much resemble the quaint isolated setting most of us have long imagined. It was instead a throbbing, well-organized commercial realm thoroughly connected with the outside world and where racial divisions grew alarmingly.

Tise was appointed Wilbur and Orville Wright Distinguished Professor at East Carolina University in 2000. *Circa 1903* is his third book on little-known aspects of the Wright brothers' North Carolina adventures. *Hidden Images in the Wright Brothers' Photographs* appeared in 2005. *Conquering the Sky* on the 1908 secret flights of the brothers followed in 2009. These are unlikely to be his last. His most recent book, *New Voyages to Carolina* (2017), was the culmination of a collaborative effort to formulate a new narrative of North Carolina's history.